The Golden Pathway Annu

A Play

John Harding
and
John Burrows

Samuel French – London
New York – Sydney – Toronto – Hollywood

ISBN 0 573 01666 6

Please see page x for further copyright information

CHARACTERS

The Officer
George Peters
Enid Peters
Michael Peters
Collins
A Chicken
Vadia
June
Miss Jones
Owen
Mr Seth
Roger
William
Lady
Mademoiselle
The Head
Girl Friend
Irishman
Magistrate
Doorman

Act I 1945–57
Act II 1957–68

THE GOLDEN PATHWAY ANNUAL

First presented at the Crucible Theatre, Sheffield, and given its first performance in London at the Mayfair Theatre on 23rd July, 1974. The play was presented by Michael Codron by arrangement with the Crucible Theatre, and in association with Robert Stigwood. The cast was as follows:

George Peters	Mark Wing-Davey
Michael Peters	John Burrows
Enid Peters **June** **Miss Jones** **William** **Lady** **Mademoiselle** **Girl Friend**	Maggie McCarthy
The Officer **Collins** **A Chicken** **Vadia** **Owen** **Mr Seth** **Roger** **The Head** **Irishman** **Magistrate** **Doorman**	John Harding

The play was directed by Ed Thomason

INTRODUCTION

When I commissioned John Harding and John Burrows to write a play, my brief to them made no specific demands as to theme or subject matter. They said they wanted to write about a boy growing up in the period from the end of the last War to the present day. I told them to go ahead.

That was about as much as I knew when the first batch of material arrived through the letterbox. It was the projected first half; a thick manuscript written rather interestingly in two distinctive hands, so that it was immediately obvious which author had written what. The structure was a loosely-linked succession of short scenes or sketches.

By coincidence John Burrows telephoned within seconds of my having quickly read this first draft. He asked me straight out what I thought about the play. Critics and audiences alike have since commented on the authors' "fine instinct for the potent, nostalgic symbol", and I remember in those first moments of trying to be articulate about the script the way my personal memories of the year after the war came so vividly into my mind. If "nostalgia" is the right word for this quality then it is nostalgia intelligently informed by a very accurate eye and ear for period detail, and a satirical wit which provokes both laughter and nods of recognition so that the constant accompanying thought to "Ah, I remember it well . . .", is, "Yes, that is exactly how it was . . .". In my own case the effect had come mainly through my deep-seated identification with the main character, Michael. After all I too was one of the post 1945 "bulge" generation, and I too had actually lived in one room with my parents in the years of austerity after the war. My mother, like Michael's mother, had scraped to make ends meet by working as a cleaner in large, expensively furnished houses in the posher end of town, and I had also watched the strange and arduous ritual of the Coronation on a newly acquired television set. My own parents had worried themselves almost to the point of hysteria about my eleven-plus examination, the first step on my personal golden pathway, or so they thought.

Subsequently, and sometime after that garbled telephone conversation with John Burrows, when the process of mounting the first production began, the thoughts which made up that first instinctive response provided significant points of departure for my treatment of the play. My own identification with Michael was not coincidental or peculiar to me. Michael was not merely a well-observed, well-written character; he was an archetype. Michael's experience in the play was representative of a generation growing up in Britain in the last twenty-five years.

Every event in the script which had sparked off a personal memory, a moment of recognition for me, would do the same to an audience—but of course it would do so in a unique way for each individual. This at least was the way I decided a production should work. It should provide the means for an audience to create their own personal, imaginative connections with Michael and his family and their "progress" down the years.

In terms of a production style this ruled out naturalism, which is the art of recreating the specific. And indeed Burrows and Harding never visualized the presentation of the play in anything but a strictly non-naturalistic style. They came up with the idea of setting the play in front of a screen on which was pasted the START-RITE Shoes advertisement depicting two children hand-in-hand stepping out on a yellow road disappearing into an ominously empty perspective. The poster slogan is: "Children's shoes have far to go. Start-rite and they'll walk happily ever after." The yellow road was continued on to the stage, so that all the action, regardless of place or time, or whether scenes were interior or exterior would be taking place on the golden pathway. This was exactly the right visual background for the play. Not only was it an ironic statement in itself, but equally important as far as I was concerned, the technical simplicity which it imposed would allow the audience this rich, imaginative and personal response to the text. Consider, for instance, the following interchange in Scene 2, when George has just arrived home after demob.

George . . . I was dead worried when you got bombed out.
Enid We lost everything George. All the wedding china, everything. This place was all I could get. It's not much.
George You made it nice though. What are the other rooms like?
Enid There aren't any other rooms George, except a little kitchen. We have to share a bathroom. And this is a Put-u-Up. It comes out quite easy. I couldn't get anything else.

If there is nothing on the stage at all except two chairs which by allusion the actress playing Enid "makes" into the Put-u-Up (and which incidentally in the previous scene have served as the officer's sports car) then the audience must imagine the specific qualities of the room, and indeed of the sports car, for themselves. These, as it were, invisible items must be coloured in by the audience in terms of their own experience.

But this would only be the starting point. I certainly did want the audience to imaginatively participate by painting in their own backdrops, flying in their own scenery, dressing and furnishing the show for themselves; but also, in doing so, I wanted them to evoke for themselves, to conjure up, a whole era and their own changing personal circumstances during that era and its aftermath—the continuing process of British life today, here and now.

★ ★ ★ ★ ★

Sit in a full theatre and you will think you see so many lines drawn from the circumference of so many ears, while the actor is in the centre.

JOHN WEBSTER, "An Excellent Actor"—*Characters 1615*

A simplified, stylized setting makes great demands of the actor who becomes the principal element of the *mise-en-scène*, the crucial link between the author and his audience. Every script is a complex and multi-layered collection of emotional and intellectual forces which only achieve their full potential when brought to life by the actor in performance. In performance an actor reveals a script by virtue of his appearance, his voice, his movement, his awareness of and attitude to his environment and to the other actors. The rehearsal process may be described as the discovery by the actor through trial and error of *the* voice, *the* movement, etc. which coheres most effectively with what is given in the text. Sometimes a gifted actor can surprise an audience with what he brings to a performance of a well-known script; this often happens with new productions of Shakespeare, for instance. Sometimes a gifted actor can reveal things in a text even to the author himself, and this can even happen when actor and author are one and the same person—as it did in the first production of *The Golden Pathway Annual*, when two of the cast of four (who between them played all the parts) were the authors themselves.

An interesting example of this is the two-handed scene at the beginning of Act II where Michael (Burrows) and his school friend Owen (Harding) are pretending to be nineteenth-century missionaries in darkest Africa. On the face of it the scene is a skilfully accurate and humorous parody of adventure story-writers such as Captain Marryat or Robert Louis Stevenson.

> **Michael** The fourth of May, eighteen hundred and ninety-four. One whole year has passed since we began our journey and oh! how this fever grips me! Without the Lord's mercy and Owen, my faithful black servant, my race would long since have ended. Of our original party there is now but left the two of us . . .

In rehearsal a closer examination revealed that a major part of the comic action of the scene was the relationship between Michael and Owen. It is clear that Michael, in the heroic role of "Father Peters" intends to dominate the play-acting, while Owen must pick up all the bit parts—the helmsman, the mutinous bos'n, etc. As the actors play the scene, Owen's attempts to get in on the game become more and more funny. Having lost the sword fight just when he thought he'd won, he tries desperately to involve himself in the next section, and when Michael soliloquizes, "Oh how this fever grips me", Owen obligingly claps two hands on Michael's shoulders—after all he can be a fever and grip as well as the next chap—Michael concedes a little to Owen's enthusiasm and seems about to involve him again: "Without the Lord's help and Owen . . ."—there is a pause here as Owen's face lights up in anticipation of perhaps being cast in a better part this time. Then Michael continues ". . . my faithful black servant". And the laugh comes, of course, on Owen's dismay. This comic tension between Michael and Owen is definitely there in the text, but it was not fully discovered and exploited until the authors looked at the scene they had written from the point of view of performers. Rivalry between Owen and Michael had, in fact, already been established in the Junior School scene in the first Act, when under the pretext of an improvised drama lesson they act out the Coronation of Elizabeth II. On the face of it, this scene simply shows the impact of the Coronation on Michael Peters, and the tiny and sometimes absurd details his seven-year-old mind has retained of the long and solemn televising of the historical occasion. When we rehearsed the scene what emerged very strongly was the favouritism bestowed on Michael by his teacher, and the jealousy this inspires in Owen, who desperately wants teacher's approval too. The resulting interplay between the boys, with each one striving for the teacher's attention, becomes the prominent comic content of this scene in performance.

Another challenge Harding and Burrows set themselves when they came to perform their own material was one that affected the other members of the cast as well, and will affect any actor who tackles the family characters in *The Golden Pathway Annual.* It is the technical challenge created by the hybrid "play/revue" format the authors chose for their material. Although there is a story-content and there are on-going characters as in a conventional play, the structure of *The Golden Pathway Annual* is a loosely connected sequence of sketches, some deliberately written for great comic effect and others, equally deliberately, pitched in a much lower key. The actors playing George and Enid, for instance, are required to play burlesque fantasy:

George Here Enid have you read this?
Enid What is it, another proclamation?
George Yes, about the king offering half his kingdom to anyone who kills the dragon. Look at this headline—K.O. DRAGON FOR FORTUNE SAYS KING . . . it's our lucky day, Enid.
Enid You don't think you could kill the dragon do you?
George Why not? They don't call me George for nothing.

and then, later in the play, genuine pathos.

George I'll put the telly on. See what old Andy Stewart's doing up at the White Heather Club.
Enid I don't want the television on. And I don't want you to go on pretending everything's all right when it's not. I want you to tell me what's happening. George, answer!
George I don't know what you want to know. Michael's got his own life to lead. He'll be all right.
Enid I'm not talking about Michael. I want to know about us.
George What about us?
Enid What's going to happen to us?
George When?
Enid When we die.

The only way for the actor to successfully render the *whole* play is to let neither the broad comic playing nor the low-key character acting dominate; both must be judged and pitched to a very delicate balance. There must be poise and awareness in the playing so that the format comes across not as an uneasy mixture but as the exhilarating and rewarding theatrical blend that it is.

The rapid succession of short scenes results in an elliptical treatment of the story content and the actor must also be wary of the dangers in this. For instance two consecutive scenes can be years apart—as when early on in the play Michael grows in the space of five lines from a twinkle in his father's eye to a two-year-old infant.

Enid There's a lovely twinkle in your eye, George.

They kiss

SCENE 3

Enid George.
George Hello, Enid.
Enid All right at work was it?
George Not too bad. (*To Michael*) And how's my little lad, eh? Come here, Michael. What, two-and-a-half years old?

As a result of this high-speed narrative method the development of character is somewhat taken for granted, and the thematic point of each short sketch, be it satirical or otherwise, is really the focus of the playwrights' attention. This means that during rehearsals actors playing the on-going character roles must work hard at building up and "realizing" their characters, so that they can manage their high-speed progress through the short scenes of the play, and the widely differing themes of the text convincingly and without confusion or inconsistency.

★ ★ ★ ★ ★

These notes are offered simply as personal reflections arising from the play's first production and I have deliberately refrained from any detailed discussion about the content of the piece. I do so confident that, in this printed form, *The Golden Pathway Annual* will speak for itself as forcefully as it did upon the stage.

ED THOMASON

COPYRIGHT INFORMATION

(See also page ii)

PRODUCTION NOTES

The Characters

The play is written for a cast of three men and one woman. One actor plays George only, the second Michael only, and the third plays all the other male roles. The actress plays all the women, including Enid.

George Peters; Enid Peters, *his wife*; **Michael Peters**, *their son*: The Peters family is a typical London working-class family, untypical in that the son gets to Grammar School and University. George and Enid are not unintelligent.
The Officer: Young, inbred, public school, plum-in-the-mouth type. Cheery and "awfully keen".
Collins: Successful, smooth, fast-talking, well-spoken con man. Wears spectacles he doesn't need. Thirtyish.
A Chicken: A chicken.
Vadia: Mean, middle-aged, snake-like business man. Heavy Swiss accent. Over-emotive and slippery, he feels under constant threat of his employees getting his money.
Owen: Schoolboy. Michael's friendly rival and henchman.
Seth: Mild, delicate, painfully polite Indian law student with a respect for all things English.
Roger: Braying, middle-class Enid Blyton gang leader. Very out-doorsy. About thirteen.
The Head: Arrogant, slithery and sadistic in the fantasy. Eccentric, bluff and hearty in reality with manic temper when crossed. Typical pompous Head.
Irishman: Stage navvy.
Magistrate: A magistrate.
Doorman: Bellowing cockney "You 'orrible little man" ex-drill sergeant with a log on his shoulder.
June: An alert secretary who has the measure of her boss.
Miss Jones: A Welsh schoolmistress.
William: Enid Blyton's Famous Five twelve-year-old-tomboy.
Lady: Mature, svelte, house-bound nymphomaniac.
Mademoiselle Ophelia: Chic young French student. Every boy's dream of the sultry Frenchwoman.
Girl Friend: A girl friend.

The Setting

Essentially just a space furnished with two wooden kitchen chairs, the playing area becomes whatever location the actors suggest.

In the end-staging of the original production a screen approximately twelve feet wide was set upstage to conceal prop table and quick change area, and provided easy access for exits and entrances around its edges. On this screen was mounted the famous "Start-rite" shoe poster, seen for many years on the London Underground Railway, depicting two small children walking away towards the horizon vanishing point of a tree-lined, sandy-coloured, country road. The perspective of the road was continued on to the stage floor, defining the playing area, which became in effect a Golden Pathway.

The Costumes

The characters are based on types, both real and fictional, that have become well-known during the period since the end of World War II, and what they wear should make them easily recognizable both in time, place and social standing.

In the original production with a cast of four, the problem of costume changes was overcome by designing a basic costume for each actor that could be quickly modified for each character he played. Of course, no attempt was made at disguise, part of the audience's enjoyment being the pleasure of watching the same person play different roles in quick succession. One point worth mentioning: neither of the schoolboys wore short trousers at any point in the play.

Furniture and Props

As mentioned above, the only furniture in the original production was two wooden chairs. More often than not, they were used as chairs, but sometimes they served as a car, or a Put-u-Up, or a sailing boat.

All the hand props were real, although the cups, glasses and saucepans were empty and appeared so to the audience.

The glass doors in Act II, Scene 2 were mimed.

The Fantasies

There are four fantasy sequences in the play, in which Michael's imagination takes over from reality. A change in lighting or other effect should distinguish these sequences.

ACT I

Scene 1

26th July 1945. Liverpool. Britain gets a socialist Government but ex-corporal George Peters finds some are more equal than others

An Officer enters, followed by George Peters with a suitcase

Officer I say! Can you give me a push?

George salutes

No need for that any more, man. We're both civilians now. You glad to be back?

George I will be when I get back down south, sir. Liverpool's new to me. I can't quite believe it is England. They talk funnier here than they did in Karachi.

Officer Peters, isn't it?

George You've remembered my name, sir. What's the trouble then, sir? No petrol? (*Indicating two chairs, which are together, representing the car*)

Officer No, I managed to wangle some juice, but the battery's gone dead on me.

George Got far to go, sir?

Officer Chelsea, actually.

George Oh! I'm Fulham. We're nearly neighbours. Well, jump in, sir. I'll give you a push.

Officer Thanks very much. (*He gets "behind the wheel"*)

George (*ready to push*) We want to get her going, don't we, sir?

Officer All set back there?

George Waiting on orders, sir.

Officer All right. Let's give it a whirl.

George attempts to push the car

George You've not still got the handbrake on, sir?

Officer (*releasing the handbrake*) My mistake.

George Right. Here we go then. (*Pushing again*) Good. Good. Let her get a speed up. Right, let it out now.

Officer lets the clutch out

Officer She's turning! Keep going! Nearly! Almost firing! Keep it up! Keep pushing!

George is exhausted. He stops pushing

George She don't want to go, does she, sir?

Officer I can't understand it.

George I think we might have flooded the carb, sir. Better give her a minute to dry out.

Officer Quite a night to lose one's pips.

George I'm not with you, sir.

Officer Demob and a Labour landslide. Equality all round.

George Oh, yes. (*Accepting the apparent invitation to sit in the passenger seat*) Of course.

Officer One day a captain, or a corporal, in a war machine. The next, just ordinary men, working side by side in a peacetime street in a country with a forward-looking Socialist government. Makes you feel good, eh, Peters?

George Pity about Churchill, though. No gratitude some people. I don't mind telling you, sir, I voted for him.

Officer You voted Tory? Didn't you read what Major Denis Healey said at the Labour conference? "The upper classes in every country are selfish, depraved, dissolute and decadent." And we've swept them out with a new broom. What are your plans?

George Just getting back to the missus'll do for now, sir. We only got married a few months before I decided to come in.

Officer You volunteered?

George Oh, yes, sir. You got a family, sir?

Officer Mother and Father. Shall we give her another go?

George No point in hanging about with two hundred miles to go is there, sir? (*He gets ready to push again*) When you're ready.

Officer Shove away.

George Keep your fingers crossed. Try her now, sir.

Officer lets the clutch out

Officer She's taking!

George Easy with the petrol, then. That's got her!

Officer Just listen to that!

George Keep the choke out, sir!

Officer Do you think she'll keep it up?

George Yes, nothing wrong with her now.

Officer Well, we'd better be off. Thanks awfully, Corporal. Goodbye.

Officer "drives" off

George is left watching him depart

Scene 2

27th July 1945. A hero's welcome and a bulge baby's begetting

Enid enters

Enid George.

George Hallo, Enid.
Enid You'd better come in.
George Yes.
Enid You look different. You've got a tan.
George Yes. On the ship coming back. Your hair's done different.
Enid Is it? Oh, yes, I had it cut. It's the style.
George It's very nice.
Enid Do you think so?
George Oh, yes. You look lovely.
Enid Put your case down, then.
George Oh, stupid! I nearly forgot. (*He takes an ornamental elephant from the case*) Here you are.
Enid What is it?
George I got it in India. It's Indian.
Enid Oh, it's nice.
George Hand-carved. One of their gods, it is. You could use it for cigarettes.
Enid Oh, I see. It opens. There's something inside.
George I had to guess the size.
Enid Stockings! Oh, George.
George I hope they're all right. Oh, Enid.

They kiss

Enid I've got lipstick on you something awful. Here, let me wipe . . .
George No. Go on. Stick some more on.
Enid Did you miss me, George?
George 'Course I missed you. I love you, don't I? I was dead worried when you got bombed out.
Enid We lost everything, George. All the wedding china. Everything. This was all I could get. It's not much.
George You've made it nice, though. What are the other rooms like?
Enid There aren't any other rooms, George, except a little kitchen. We have to share the bathroom. (*Indicating the chairs*) And that's a Put-u-Up. It comes out quite easy. I couldn't get anywhere else, George.
George No, it's lovely. Hey! (*Indicating his demob suit*) What do you think of the whistle? Not bad, is it? Good fit.
Enid It's nice, George.
George They give you that. Here, how are you off for clothes?
Enid Not bad. I mean considering the ration. I go careful, you know.
George First thing tomorrow, girl, we're going to buy you a complete new outfit. Whatever you want.
Enid That'd be lovely, George, but I haven't got any coupons.
George You don't need 'em, girl.
Enid Black market, George?
George The war's nearly over, love. Anyway it's a celebration. I want to get you something. Something nice.
Enid Could I really have just what I wanted?
George Whatever your heart takes a fancy to.

Enid Oh, George, I do love you.

The Lights go out

George Hello.
Enid It's only the meter gone.
George That's convenient.
Enid Have you got a penny, George?
George Let's leave 'em off, eh?
Enid No. Don't be daft, George. I've got some sausage rolls and things for you over there.
George I'm not hungry.
Enid George. Stop acting the goat, go on.
George All right, then. Where's the meter?
Enid Over by the door.
George I've just remembered, I've got another surprise for you. Hang on.

The Lights come on. George, facing upstage, undoes his belt and pulls up his shirt

Enid Here, George. What are you doing?
George Won't be a moment.
Enid What is it?
George Don't you like it?
Enid I wasn't expecting it.
George It's a tattoo: "George and Enid. True Love".
Enid Is it permanent?
George 'Course it is. It's a tattoo.
Enid What did you want to do that for?
George 'Cause I love you.
Enid But suppose I should die or something, you'd be stuck with it forever.
George Don't say such things, Enid. Don't you ever die. I love you, Enid.
Enid I love you too. Kiss me, George. Shall I show you how to do the Put-u-Up?
George Yeah. Come on then.
Enid There's a lovely twinkle in your eye, George.

They kiss and hold their position while Michael enters for the next scene

Scene 3

1948. The Age of Austerity

Michael enters and sits on the floor

George and Enid come out of their embrace. Several years have passed

Enid George.
George Hello, Enid.
Enid All right at work, was it?

George Not too bad. And now how's my little lad then, eh? Come here, Michael. What, two-and-a-half years old? You're strong as a lion. Let me feel your muscles. Cor, like iron. I wouldn't like to have a fight with you.
Enid Don't tease him, George, he's only a baby.
George Who's a clever little lad? (*Lifting the child in the air*) Whee! But I bet you don't know where I keep my slippers.
Enid You're so artful, George.
George Train 'em young. Come here, son, and say hello to your dad.
Enid He carried my shopping all up the road today, didn't you, Michael?
George You been carrying your mum's shopping? I'll have to give you some wages, won't I? Come and see what I've got for you in my bag. What are they, Michael? Lovely big cakes!
Enid Not before his tea.
George Have it after your tea, though, eh? That's right. I've got something for you too, Enid. Bit of butter and sugar.
Enid Oh, that's nice, George, lovely!
George I got 'em off a bloke at work. I did him a favour. I lent him the firm's lorry for the weekend.

Enid exits with Michael

Scene 4

1951. George and Enid ensure Michael's future for less than the price of ten cigarettes a week

Enid (*off*) I think that was a knock, George.
George Well, I don't know who it could be. I've taken the rent down.
Enid (*off*) You gonna answer it, then?

Collins enters with a briefcase and questionnaire clipboard

George answers the door to him

George Yes?
Collins Good-evening, Mr and Mrs George Peters?
George Yes. That's right.
Collins You have a little boy, Michael?
George Yes. What's the trouble, then?
Collins Oh, no trouble at all, Mr Peters. Quite the opposite. My name is Collins. I'm from the Institute for the Educationally Aware. We're conducting a survey amongst the parents of bright children in the area. I wonder if you'd be prepared to help us?
George You'd better come in, then.
Collins What a snug little home.
George Yes. We're looking for something a bit bigger.
Collins It's terrible finding a house, isn't it? I had to search for ages.
Enid (*off*) What is it, George?
George It's about Michael, Enid. Gentleman wants to ask some questions.

Enid (*off*) Oh. Would he like some tea?
Collins Please don't trouble yourself, Mrs Peters.

Enid enters

Enid Oh, it's no trouble.
Collins Thank you very much.
George This is my wife. This is Mr——
Collins Collins. Institute for the Educationally Aware.
George Sit yourself down.
Collins I just want to ask you both some questions concerning Michael's future.
Enid Oh, yes.
Collins If I could just get some details first. When was Michael born?
Enid Just after midnight.
George No, he means the date, Enid.
Enid Sixth May nineteen forty-six.
Collins So he'll be five next month. Has he started school yet?
George Yes. Easter he started.
Collins Does Michael seem to enjoy it?
Enid Oh yes. He loves his school. He's got a lovely young teacher, but she's not silly.
George He doesn't say much about it, 'cause he's a quiet boy, you know . . .
Collins Sensitive?
George Yes, that's it. But he definitely likes it.
Collins Well, enjoying school is the first step in a good career, I always think, and indeed this is backed up by our findings. This brings us to the questionnaire proper. Lovely tea, Mrs Peters. Have you given any thought as to how your child's school career might be enhanced by your educational role as parents, bearing in mind the growing emphasis throughout industry on mental rather than manual skills?
Enid Oh, yes.
George We both want him to do well.
Collins Yes. Have you taken any steps yourselves to ensure Michael's success with suitable educational stimulants in the home?
George Stimulants? Well, I think he should relax a bit at home. I mean, he's only five. We don't want to flog him . . .
Collins No, quite, Mr Peters. We don't want to make Jack a dull boy, ha-ha, but that's just my point. I think the next question takes us further on this topic. Ah, yes. Would you agree with Winston Churchill——
George Yes.
Collins —when he says that the following are important to Michael's development: history, stories of the world's great leaders, explorers, scientists, artists and their achievements, well-written, imaginatively illustrated stories from the classics made suitable for children but retaining the grandeur of English prose at its best?
Enid All that's very important, I think.
Collins Well, have you heard of *The Golden Pathway Annual*, the Children's Companion Books published by the Institute for the Educationally

Aware? I have a specimen copy here. *The Golden Pathway Annual* is not just one book. It's a series of ten, a whole programme of learning, recommended by leading educationalists, which arrive annually on the child's birthday, gift-wrapped with a card, and which become to the child a friendly guide right from early childhood into his teens.

Enid They get them on their birthday?

Collins Yes. Something for the child to look forward to each year. May Sixth in Michael's case. We find that five is a good age to start with the first volume concerned with nursery rhymes, fairy tales and so on, going on in the other volumes through Mythology, The World In Which We Live, Animal Stories, Great Discoveries, and here and there modern adventure tales in which the heroes are, themselves, children. You can hold it up by one page, it won't fall apart.

Enid That sounds nice.

George It's very nice. I must say, I'm impressed, you know. But how much does it cost?

Collins What price do you put on Michael's future, Mr Peters? A packet of cigarettes?

George Ha. A lot more than that.

Collins Well, *The Golden Pathway Annual* costs less than the price of ten cigarettes a week. A few pence in fact.

Enid I've been wanting him to cut down his smoking anyway.

George Well, I think, yes. What do you say, Enid?

Enid Oh, I think yes, too.

George In that case, yes, we'd like him to have them. Will it come for his birthday, then?

Collins Yes, indeed, Mr Peters. I think you've made a very wise decision. I know my own children have benefited enormously. If you'll just sign there. My local representative will call each week for the subscription. I've got all the details, and I'll leave you your membership card, your half of the agreement, and this explanatory leaflet. Good-night, Mr Peters, Mrs Peters. I wish Michael the greatest success. I'll see myself out.

Collins exits

Enid I've been wondering what to get him for his birthday.

Enid exits

Scene 5

1951. For the young child the world is full of dangers. Not least of these is the possessive parent

The Chicken enters, clucking; and Michael and Enid enter with saucepan of chicken food

Enid I do think they're funny animals.

George There's nothing funny about our chickens. Is there, Michael?

Enid I don't like them. Watch your fingers, Michael.

George He's all right. Leave him be.

Enid I don't want him losing his fingers. Fancy him going through life with a handicap like that!

George Don't put your fingers through the wire, Michael, your mother's worried about your career as a concert pianist.

Enid You think you're so funny, George Peters, don't you?

George Well, you can't be forever watching over them, Enid; you've got to leave them to it sometime.

Enid He's only a baby.

George He goes to school, doesn't he?

Enid I suppose you'll be getting him a little part-time job next?

George You'd make a good hen yourself, Enid.

Enid Anyway, why shouldn't Michael play the piano? You're always going on about how musical your family are.

George No reason whatsoever.

Enid That's your trouble. You don't take a pride in Michael.

George We'll give them their food now, shall we, boy?

Enid That's right; you go off with your son.

George Enid, the boy and I are going to go inside the run and give the chickens their food, about six foot away. We are not going off together. Come with us if you want or stay there, it doesn't really matter, we won't exactly be on the other side of the world, will we?

Enid When are you going to K.I.L.L. one for the lady downstairs?

The Chicken hears this and is alarmed

George What?

Enid You heard.

George What you spelling it for?

Enid Because he's a child.

George Well, he's eaten enough of them, Enid. I don't suppose he thinks they get into the oven of their own accord.

The Chicken is appalled

Enid You are a very cruel man.

The Chicken agrees

George Blimey! You're the one who pulls their feathers out and chops their heads off.

Enid Yes, when they're dead.

George Yes, well you're an accessory then, aren't you? So if I'm a murderer, so are you. Come on, Michael, let's give them their food. What are you crying for, Michael?

Michael, upset by his parents bickering, is in silent tears

Enid Has that chicken bit him, George?

George Don't be daft. What are you crying for, son?

Enid What's the matter, Michael? Tell your mum.

George I think you better take him inside, Enid. Something's upset him.
Enid It's those chickens. I told you they were funny.

Michael and Enid exit. The Chicken resumes clucking as George lures it upstage with food, then kicks it off. George exits

Scene 6

1951. Michael wants to be Jack the Giant Killer and make his mum and dad rich

George, Enid and Michael enter. They bring with them a birthday cake with five candles, the gift-wrapped Golden Pathway Annual, *and a newspaper*

George and Enid sing "Happy Birthday" to Michael

George One big blow.
Enid And wish.

Michael blows out the candles

Lovely. Open this one the postman brought, Michael. (*Feigning ignorance for Michael's sake*) I wonder what it can be?
George It's that *Golden Pathway Annual.*
Enid Oh, George!
Michael It's a book. I can't read yet.
Enid I'll read it to you. "Once upon a time, there was a little boy called Michael, who lived with his mother and father in a very tiny hovel and they were very, very poor. What little money they had they earned by selling brooms."

Fantasy begins

George I earned a little money today, Enid. I sold a broom.
Enid How much did you get for it?
George Only a farthing.
Enid Well, there's no money about is there, George? The country is still getting over the war, isn't it?
George No, it's not that. I put it down to this dragon.
Enid What, the one that's stolen the king's daughter?
George Yes, the one that's kidnapped the princess and says he's going to eat her unless everyone in the land gives him half their food each week. I mean, as long as they're giving half what they earn each week away to the dragon, they're not going to have any money left over to buy our brooms, are they?
Enid No, of course not. I think it's terrible the way some dragons carry on, picking on poor helpless princesses. She's a lovely-looking girl, too; when you think it was only last Christmas we were listening to her on the wireless.

George Never mind about her, what about us? If it wasn't for her we wouldn't have to give half our food away. Chuck us over the paper, Enid, let's have a look what's on at the flicks. Take our minds off things a bit.

Enid You know, even if he hadn't got the princess we'd still have to give him our food because of that fire up his nose.

George Here, have you read this?

Enid What is it? Another proclamation?

George Yes, about the king offering half his kingdom to anyone who kills the dragon. Look, 'K.O. DRAGON FOR FORTUNE SAYS KING.'

Michael (*as young hero*) Can I see, Father?

George It's our lucky day. That fortune's as good as ours, Enid.

Enid You don't think you could kill the dragon, do you?

George Why not? They don't call me George for nothing.

Michael (*as hero*) It says here whoever kills the dragon will also receive the hand of the princess in marriage.

George (*eagerly*) Well, that settles it then.

Enid George, what do you mean, that settles it?

George (*getting out of it*) I can't go, can I? Not if once you've killed the dragon you have to marry the princess. I mean I'm already spoken for, aren't I, love?

Enid George.

George You're the only one for me, Enid.

Enid We could half do with the money, though.

Michael (*as hero*) Mother and Father, I shall go!

Enid Oh, no, Michael!

George That's an idea, son. Enid, where's that fire bucket and stirrup pump we had during the blitz.

They are handed to George from off stage

Oh, here they are! You'll find these very useful, Michael. Throw the sand in his eyes and squirt water up his nose. I'd come with you, son, but we can't both marry the princess, can we?

Michael takes the bucket and pump and kisses his mother farewell

Enid So, Michael, having kissed his mother and father farewell, set off on his quest to kill the dragon, rescue the princess and win his just reward. A song put heart in his step and in his right hand he held the magic weapons his father had given him. And this is the song Michael sang:

Michael (*singing*) I shall kill the dragon
I shall stab him in the head.
Everyone will be happy,
When the dragon's dead.

All repeat twice and during the last verse they exit, dancing

Scene 7

1952. George and the Dragon. George asks for a rise and gets fired

Vadia and June, with a cup of tea, enter

June One of the men, George Peters, wants to see you.
Vadia Thank you, June, my little Peaches and Cream. Come and have a little sit on my knee.
June Someone might see, Mr Vadia.
Vadia Call me Bruno.
June Someone might see, Bruno.
Vadia Who is going to see? I am the boss. It's my factory. Come and sit on my knee.

She does so. Vadia drinks the tea

June I don't know how you can drink your tea like that.
Vadia Like what?
June Without any milk in it. Don't you find it strong?
Vadia No, I find it cheaper. June, I've got a little proposition to put to you. How would you like to spend the weekend with me playing golf?
June I can't play golf.
Vadia I'll teach you.
June I've got nothing to wear.
Vadia So much the better.
June What about your wife?
Vadia She's in Switzerland, changing her nose.
June What for?
Vadia Another one, more expensive.
June I couldn't afford to come and play golf.
Vadia Have a little something out of next week's wages. You see, there's nothing you can say that will put me off.
June George Peters wants to see you about a pay rise.

Vadia is crestfallen

June exits. George enters

Vadia George, it's good to see you.
George I just wanted a word with you for a minute, Mr Vadia.
Vadia I don't say that to everyone, George. Some people I couldn't care less about, but you, it's good to see. Because you are a special person—you have contentment. There's nothing you need, and you're looking so well. You're getting fatter.
George You don't pay me enough for that, Mr Vadia.
Vadia And always joking! You see, you're happy in your work.
George Mr Vadia, now that the firm is on its feet again and things are looking up, I think it's about time I had a pay rise.
Vadia (*feigning sudden pain*) Would you excuse me one moment while I take this pill?

George You under the weather?

Vadia It's nothing. Just worry.

George Worry about what?

Vadia My wife, George. She's in a clinic in Zurich. The doctors say there is not much hope she'll pull through. They don't know what's the matter with her and I don't know how I am going to afford the treatment with all the financial pressures I'm under just now. But that's not your burden. Thank goodness some people can be happy in the world.

George Don't worry, she'll be all right.

Vadia I'm not so sure. But don't you stay here listening to me being depressed. (*Showing George the door*) I'm sure there is plenty of work you want to be doing.

George Mr Vadia, it struck me this morning while I was cleaning your Austin Princess . . .

Vadia Tell me, George, how long is it since we've been friends together?

George I've worked for you since nineteen thirty-seven.

Vadia Fourteen years. We were younger then!

George Apart from the war, that is.

Vadia I always thought it was such a pity about the war. I wish I could have gone with you, to have all the fun fighting, but my country was not involved. I'm Swiss, you see. Instead I had to stay here and expand the factory. It wasn't easy, with all my best boys gone. But somehow I managed. How, I don't know, with Jerry doodle-bombing on us. I did it for you, George, so you'd have a job to come back to. I didn't do it for myself, George, it was for you. (*Feigning breakdown*) I used to lie in bed at night wondering just how many of my babies would come back.

George I promised myself I'd ask for a rise today.

Vadia Don't make me angry, George, not when I'm upset.

George I can't manage on the money you're giving me.

Vadia Don't threaten me, George, not when I'm angry.

George I must have an extra twelve-and-six.

Vadia This is so hurtful.

George I'm sorry, Mr Vadia, I didn't mean to hurt you.

Vadia Well, you have.

George I didn't mean to.

Vadia All right, George, I believe you. And in the circumstances I'm prepared to do you a favour.

George That's very decent of you.

Vadia Yes. I'm prepared to go on as if you never said those things.

George No, I can't do that. It's either the rise or I give my notice in.

Vadia OK, Peters, I am the boss. You don't talk to me like that. I fire you. Go to Wages. Get your cards. I never want to speak to you again.

George exits

Is that what we fought the war for? A society based on greed?

Vadia exits

Scene 8

3rd June 1953. A Primary School Teacher takes her two small pupils to the Coronation and makes them loyal subjects

Miss Jones, Michael and Owen enter. Miss Jones sits upstage, facing her class which consists of the two boys, sitting crosslegged, and the audience

Miss Jones Did you all have a lovely time yesterday? That's good. Lots of nice things to eat? I see Michael is wearing a lovely new hat. Did you make that yourself? Come out and show everyone, Michael. That's it. Now red, white and blue are the same colours as the Union Jack, aren't they? Did you wear that special hat yesterday, Michael?

Michael Yes, I put it on to watch the television.

Miss Jones Did anybody else see the Coronation on television? Oh you seem to be the only one Michael, that's lucky for you. You can tell us everything you saw in a minute. But first—what happened yesterday morning, before the Queen went to Westminster Abbey? Doesn't anybody know? What news did the Queen get for a present when she read the papers? Yes, Owen?

Owen Somebody climbed Mount Everest.

Miss Jones That's right. And why is Mount Everest so important?

Michael It's the highest mountain in the world. It's twenty-nine thousand, and two feet high.

Miss Jones That's good. Fancy you knowing that, Michael. And what is that in miles? Divide twenty-nine thousand, and two by how many feet in a mile? Yes, Owen.

Owen Five thousand, two hundred and eighty.

Miss Jones Good. So do your long division. Who's going to be first with the answer.

Owen Five remainder two thousand, six hundred and two.

Miss Jones Very quick, Owen. Did everybody get the same answer? Five miles and two thousand, six hundred and two feet. Wasn't that a lovely present for Queen Elizabeth to have the Union Jack put up that high for the Coronation?

Owen The wind tore it to pieces in a few hours, miss.

Miss Jones Well, never mind, Owen, it's the thought that counts. Now, Michael, (*indicating him to come out to the front of the class*) what did you see on the television?

Michael Lots of soldiers and horses and bands and coaches, and then they went into the church and prayed a lot and the Queen had to promise to be a good Queen and the Prince Philip sat beside her and they put the crown on her head, and then everyone else put their crowns on.

Miss Jones Yes, yes, go on.

Michael And then they waited a bit and then they changed crowns because one was too heavy with jewels and would give her a headache and she got in the Coronation coach with men walking beside it and went home to the palace.

Miss Jones What colour was the queen's coach?

Michael Grey.

Miss Jones Well, it was grey on the television, Michael, but what colour was it really? What colour is best for a queen?

Michael Gold.

Miss Jones That's right. A lovely golden coach. And what did the Queen do in the coach?

Michael Smiled and waved at the people. (*He demonstrates Elizabeth II's wave*)

Miss Jones And what did the people do?

Owen They waved and shouted back.

Miss Jones Yes they went mad, didn't they?

The Boys get carried away in their shouting and waving

That's enough, settle down. Would you like to act out the Coronation part? All right then, who's going to be Queen?

The Boys are both keen

Well, I don't know really. I mean we need a girl don't we, and you're all boys in this class. So who could it be?

The Boys You, miss!

Miss Jones Don't be silly. Oh, all right then. And what do I have to wear?

Owen A dress.

Miss Jones Yes, Owen, but what kind of dress?

Michael A golden dress.

Miss Jones That's right. With a very full skirt all gold and jewels and lace, and quite a tight nipped-in waist and diamonds on the bodice, and a beautiful long velvet train trimmed with ermine and ladies-in-waiting just to look after it. Well. Let's do the procession to the Abbey first. Everybody stand up quietly.

They stand up noisily

Quietly! Come on, now, fingers on lips! And now walk slowly, slowly, very dignified, behind me round the classroom. That's it, now step carefully over the painting book. Remember what a holy place we're in. Where's Prince Philip?

Michael Here.

Miss Jones And is somebody holding my train?

Owen Yes.

Miss Jones Make sure it doesn't drag. We don't want to get it dirty. And what do I do now, Michael? All right, fingers off lips.

Michael Pray.

Miss Jones And then what?

Michael You sit on the throne.

Miss Jones Good. And what's under the throne? Leave the hamsters alone, Owen, they're not hurting you are they? What's under the throne?

Owen A big stone.

Miss Jones That's right. It's the stone of Scone. Scone is a place in Scotland. Now what do I do?

Michael You hold the sceptres in your hands, and the bishops do a lot of things.
Miss Jones Well, you be the bishops, Michael,

Michael gets an empty school milk bottle

What are you doing with the milk bottle, Michael? It's not playtime yet.
Michael It's the golden eagle with the oil in it. I have to put some on a golden spoon and anoint you with it.
Miss Jones Everybody can do that then. Carefully hold your golden eagles in one hand, and your golden spoons in the other. Now carefully pour a little oil into the spoon, I don't want to see any spilt, and then carefully pour the oil over your heads. All right. Now do I get the crown? Quickly get a hat from the dressing-up box.

Michael gets a hat

That's it. Now reach up high, and slowly, slowly down.

Michael lifts the hat high above his head and lowers it with agonizing slowness

Michael God save the Queen! Ta ra tara tata. Hurray!
Miss Jones That's lovely. Now all the peers of the realm can put on their coronets.

The Boys try to prevent one another from getting to the hat box first

Don't fight over them, there's plenty to go round! Hands on heads! Go on, Michael.
Michael Prince Philip has to kneel in front of you and promise allegiance and to obey you.
Miss Jones You can do that then.

The Boys kneel down on either side of her

Michael I promise to obey you and give my allegiance.
Owen Me too.
Miss Jones Good. That was lovely. Thank you, Michael. Now you can be horses and soldiers and peers of the realm in the playground. Off you go, my lovely big soldiers.

The Boys exit marching, followed by Miss Jones

Scene 9

1955. Two ardent fans of Winston Churchill exchange their souvenirs of the great man

Enid, George and Michael enter. Michael sits reading the G.P.A. *until Mr Seth's entrance*

George Listen to him go on, Enid. I'm not sure we should have let that room, you know.

Enid Don't be daft, George. How could we find the mortgage if we weren't taking someone in? What you earn driving for Zernberg's doesn't go far.

George I'm doing all right. Zernberg's is one of the top dry-cleaning firms in North London.

Enid Anyway he's very quiet usually; it's only when he gets one of his spells it gets a bit awkward. If he wants to perfect his English, George, you've got to expect him to practise. He'll have to make speeches in court, George, before the judge and jury. So he's got to practise.

George But why does it always have to be Churchill he practises on? If I've heard "I've nothing to offer you but blood, sweat, toil and tears" once, I've heard it a thousand times. It puts me off my dinner, Enid. Then he keeps asking me whether it sounds like Churchill. I never know what to say. I mean how can a little Indian from Bombay sound like Churchill? It's ridiculous.

Enid It's your own fault for telling him you and Winston were friends.

George Now I didn't say that, Enid.

Enid That's the impression you like to give.

George Do I or do I not pick up Winston Spencer Churchill's dry cleaning from 10 Downing Street every other Friday?

Enid Yes, George.

George Have I or have I not got one of his initialled handkerchiefs in the top drawer of our tallboy?

Enid Yes, George.

George Have I or have I not got a Coronation mug full of his cigar butts?

Enid Yes, George.

George So I've got some right to talk about him with a little more intimate knowledge than most people.

Enid Well, he always pays his rent on time and he treats me very respectful. Makes me feel quite a lady. Especially those little bows and Michael likes him, don't you, Michael?

Michael What?

Enid Mr Seth. You like him, don't you?

Michael He's all right.

George Well, I haven't got anything against him, Enid. You know that. Don't forget I was out in India, I've seen 'em on home ground.

Enid Well then don't go on about him practising.

George Here. He's stopped.

Enid He heard you, George.

George He never.

Enid He's coming down. Listen.

George He can't have heard me.

Mr Seth enters

Mr Seth Good-evening, Mr Peters. Good-evening, Master Michael. Good-evening, Mummy. I hope you will forgive this unbidden intrusion upon your privacy, but I wished to consult with Mr Peters on a point of English grammar which has landed pell-mell in my path.

George Oh that's all right, Mr Seth. What's your problem?

Mr Seth It is a question of the correct preposition to use after the word "different". Is it different "to" or different "from"?

George Now let me think. That's a teaser. Different "than", isn't it?

Mr Seth Oh. That differs with what I've got in my book.

George Well, it's different according to what book you've got.

Mr Seth Thank you. Tell me, Mr Peters, how is the Prime Minister of late?

George Much the same. He's not getting any younger of course. Here, I've got something for you, Mr Seth. (*He brings out a cigar from his pocket*) There you are.

Mr Seth What is it?

George It's one of Winston's. It's a cigar butt.

Mr Seth Please go on.

George Eh?

Mr Seth It's a cigar, but, what?

George It's a cigar, but most of it's been smoked. Just a memento. I thought you might like it.

Mr Seth But I don't want it.

George No, don't be bashful. You take it. It's nothing to me.

Mr Seth Your friend the Prime Minister, Winston Churchill, gave you this?

George Yes. He said "You might have a friend that'd want that, George. Little souvenir. Feel free to do what you want with it."

Mr Seth Then I accept. Thank you.

George That's all right. We're a Commonwealth after all. Friendship between the nations.

Mr Seth Yes indeed. As the great man himself has said "Here in this country we know that no dark designs are harboured by our government against the peace or well-being of any country. There may be mistakes, there may be muddles, but no dark designs are harboured by any British Prime Minister or Foreign Secretary".

George Yes. I tell you what, Mr Seth. I might have some other little thing, a handkerchief, that you might want to see.

Mr Seth Please.

George No, it's no trouble.

George exits

Enid Well. I expect you could do with a cup of tea, Mr Seth, I'll put the kettle on.

Enid exits

Michael My dad doesn't really know Mr Churchill.

Mr Seth Well, not to worry, Michael. I think it gives him pleasure to pretend sometimes. Where is the harm in that?

Michael and Mr Seth exit

Scene 10

Summer 1956. Bognor Regis. The Peters family try to have a holiday

Enid and George enter with deckchairs, followed by Michael

Enid George, how much further have I got to carry this deckchair?
George I just want to get beyond that big sewer pipe, Enid, love.
Michael I'll carry it for you, Mum.
Enid Just a minute, Michael. George, this'll do me nicely.
George No, it's not sheltered here. There's too much wind. We want to get that pipe at the back of us.
Enid If you wanted to be by that pipe why didn't you park the car near it instead of making us traipse the whole length of the beach all over these pebbles.
George You can't get deckchairs down the pipe end.
Michael You could have put the deckchairs on top of the car, Dad.
Enid Yes, that's it, Michael. Why didn't you think of that, George?
George What makes you think I didn't. For your information, I've only just painted the top of the car with rubber solution to stop the sunroof leaking.
Enid You did that ages ago.
George Well, it takes a long while to dry. Anyway, what would I have used to tie them on with, Enid?
Enid Michael?
Michael What?
Enid Not what, Michael. Pardon.
Michael Pardon, Mum.
Enid What should your dad have used to tie the deckchairs on with?
Michael Well, rope.
George I could have borrowed yours could I, son?
Michael No, I haven't got any.
Enid You mean to say you didn't bring any rope, George?
George No, Enid, I also forgot the climbing boots and pickaxes.
Enid Most people have a bit of rope in their car, George.
Michael You could have knotted the towels together, Dad.
Enid Yes, that's it, Michael. Why didn't you think of that, George?
George I don't know, Enid. Come on, let's sit here then.
Enid I thought you wanted to be out of the wind.
George That was a long time ago and this'll do me.
Enid I'm not going to sit here if you're going to sulk about it, George. I'd rather go on walking up and down the beach all day if you're going to show off about it.
George Enid, this is meant to be a holiday. Let's try and enjoy it shall we? (*After several disastrous attempts he succeeds in erecting his deckchair*) Put your mother's deckchair up for her, Michael.

Michael does so instantly. George and Enid sit down to enjoy the sun. Michael remains standing

All right, Enid?

Enid Do you want to put your swimming costume on, Michael?
Michael Not yet.
Enid Why not?
Michael I just don't, not yet.
Enid You won't get brown like that.
George Put your swimming costume on, Michael. Get yourself a nice tan.
Enid Go on, Michael, what are you waiting for? Put a towel round you. Or just quickly take your trousers down and slip your trunks on.

She attempts to take his trousers off, Michael resists

Won't take a minute. No-one's going to want to look at your little bottom. Look at that little boy, he's not bothered. Oh, please yourself then. We bring you all this way and that's how grateful you are. We might as well be at home.

Michael sits on the beach

George Want something to do, Michael? Count how many bits of tar you can see.
Enid Or find yourself a little friend.
George I'll go over and get us a beach tray in a minute, Enid. Shall I get you an ice-cream, Michael?
Michael Yes, please.
Enid We've only just had breakfast.
George Well, the landlady's breakfasts don't fill you up, do they? And she can't make a decent cup of tea to save her life.
Enid Oh yes, but you can't blame her for that, though. I mean, it's the water they have down here. It's only London water that makes a good cup of tea.
George It's not that, Enid. She's using powdered milk.
Enid You enjoying yourself, Michael?
Michael Yes, thank you. I think I'll go for a walk up to the pipe and back.
George That's it, son. Don't feel tied to us, you do what you want to.
Enid Why don't you throw your ball about?

Michael exits

I think I felt a drop of rain then. Is it raining, George?
George I think you might be right. We better get up to that shelter by the winter gardens.
Enid What about the deckchairs?
George I'll try to get the money back on them later. Where's Michael?
Enid He's down by that pipe. Look at him getting inside it! Call him, George.

Enid exits, holding her deckchair above her head

George Michael! Michael! Your mother and me are going. Come on, it's starting to rain. You'll get soaked. Michael, we're going to the shelter. Leave that stuff alone. It is not seaweed.

George exits

SCENE 11

1957. "And the hopes of the fathers shall be visited upon the heads of the sons." A pep talk

Michael enters and sits reading the G.P.A. *A knock on Michael's bedroom door*

Michael Come in, Dad.

George enters

George It's a proper little den you've got up here! What are you doing then? A bit of reading?

Michael Yes. It's a chapter on foreign stamps.

George Good. That is good. Well, stop that for a moment, Michael, if you can, because your mum and I want to have a bit of a chat with you. (*He sits*) Come on, Enid.

Enid enters

Enid Hello, Michael.

George That's it. Now what we wanted to talk to you about, son, is . . .

Enid We wanted to have a proper talk with you, Michael.

George Now that you're a bit older we think you're ready to think seriously about it.

Enid I'm sure you know what we mean.

George It's about your schoolwork, son.

Enid It's about your exam, Michael, about your eleven-plus.

Michael looks away and George takes this opportunity to start to move his chair nearer to Michael, Enid following. Michael looks back and George has to stop at the point he has reached. The scene continues in this way like the children's game "Granny's footsteps"

George You know we've always tried to do our best for you, Michael, and we know you appreciate what we've done for you. Because for us it's always been the case of, "If you can't help your own child in this world, who can you help?"

Enid Not that we're saying we've been any better than any other parents.

George No, we're not saying that. But I think we're a team, all of us, we help one another, that's all.

Enid What your dad means, Michael, is that we're a family.

George That's what I'm trying to say, son, we're a family. (*"Granny's footsteps"*) You see, Michael, when I was at school not everyone took the eleven-plus.

Enid They didn't even call it the eleven-plus then, did they, George? So it shows you how far we're going back.

George When I was at school they only let the bright ones take it who the teacher picked. So if you did get picked you were very lucky.

Enid And your dad did get picked, Michael.

George Yes, I got picked. But when I told my father, he said he didn't want me to take it because if I passed, it would have meant me staying on at school after I was fourteen.
Enid And his father wanted him to go out to work and bring some money home.
George He was a bit silly like that. What we're trying to say is we know how important it is for you to have your parents behind you.

"Granny's footsteps." George and Enid are now very close to Michael

Michael, this is a wonderful opportunity for you. So you make sure you take it, because I don't want you to end up like me.
Enid Not that there's anything wrong with your dad.
George No, there's nothing wrong with working with your hands, nothing wrong at all, but I've seen it, time after time, how the blokes with the qualifications and the letters after their names always get preference over blokes like me.
Enid You see, if you pass, Michael, you'll go to the grammar school and you'll get on and be able to do all the things we never had the chance to do.
George Which is why it's so important, son.
Enid But we'd always love you, Michael, whatever school you went to.
George That goes without saying.
Enid (*kneeling*) One thing, Michael, is that I've borrowed some eleven-plus practice papers from Mr Robertson who I work for. (*She produces practice papers*) He says if you had a little look at them beforehand they'd stand you in good stead.
George (*kneeling*) We've had a word with your teacher too, Michael, and he says you could go to the grammar school, if you tried, because you're doing very well. So start doing some of these exam papers at home, to help you, son.
Enid We just want you to know we're right behind you.
George There's nothing we wouldn't do to help you pass this exam. So I think that's all we wanted to say, really.
Michael Don't worry, Dad.
George Good lad. I know you'll do your best anyway.
Enid I'll put the kettle on.

Enid exits. George returns his chair to its original position and exits

Michael (*calling after his father*) Dad! Would you like to see a picture of a Nicaragua triangle?

Michael kneels down and studies the eleven-plus practice papers

Scene 12

1957. Michael catches a thief with The Famous Five, but their enemies aren't his enemies

Fantasy begins

Roger enters

Roger Hello, have you been thrown by your pony? I'm quite good at setting sprained ankles.
Michael No, I'm all right.
Roger Oh dear. What do you want to do then? We could Indian wrestle if you like, till William gets here with the picnic and the new torch batteries.
Michael Who's William?
Roger William's my cousin. Her real name's Wilhemena, but she's got a lot of pluck for a girl, so we call her William. I've got some mint cake here if you'd like. My name's Roger.
Michael I've read about you, and William, in *The Golden Pathway Annual.*
Roger Jolly good. We do have some pretty good adventures, don't we? We're down here at Aunt Mary's cottage for the hols as usual, but apart from some good walks and a trip round the island with Sam the fisherman, nothing much has happened yet.
Michael Where's Herbert the dog?
Roger That's the worst of it. You know how he loves to go rabbiting? Well some nasty sort put a snare down and Herbert got caught. He's laid up at the vet's at the moment. Aunt Mary took him into Borchester, so we're pretty much on our own. We shall miss his sensitive nose and warning barks. I don't suppose you can lead us to a mystery of some sort?
Michael I don't think so.
Roger No unshaven men, gypsies, treasure, or fresh fires where you wouldn't expect them?
Michael No.
Roger Never mind, you're bound to be involved somehow, or I wouldn't have met you. You can take Herbert's place for a day or two,

Michael plays being the dog

then we'll still be the Terrific Three—there used to be more of us, of course. I do wish William would hurry up with lunch, this fresh air has given me quite an appetite.
William (*off*) Roger! Roger! Where are you?
Roger Over here, William! Is anything the matter?

William enters with a picnic basket and dry-cleaning ticket

William I've found something! Oh, hello.
Roger William, this is our new Herbert.
William Oh good! The butcher gave me a super big bone: it would be a pity to waste it.
Roger But what have you found?
William It's some sort of ticket. Look. There are perforations where it's been torn out of a book or something, and there's something written in indelible pencil in terrible handwriting, and then a price, look: two and ninepence.

Roger Gracious! It could be anything! Well done, William. You're nearly as good as a boy after all! And see, there are some figures on the back written in the same indelible pencil: twelve R twenty-one L three R four L. I wonder what it could mean?

William There were some footprints on the ground where I found it, just down by the stile leading to the village school.

Roger Right-o. I'll go and take some plaster casts and have a think. You start lunch while they're setting, and I'll be back in a trice.

Roger exits

William Isn't this exciting! You're sure you don't mind being Herbert?

Michael No, not at all.

William It means I'm your master and I worry awfully about you being poisoned and things, but you can chase rabbits and bark as if you understand and growl at unsavoury tramps and I've got this lovely big bone.

Michael Woof! What have you got for lunch?

William What we always have: some loaves of new bread, a delicious meat pie, some lovely red tomatoes, a couple of tins of cool pineapple chunks, three jars of scrumptious jam, a pot of clover honey, some lean ham, slabs of Aunt Mary's home-made fruit cake, and gorgeous ginger beer to wash it down with. That should make a good lunch for hungry children! I'm ravenous! And don't you worry, Herbert, I left a note explaining that we only took it from the larder because we were jolly hungry and likely to have an adventure, so it's not stealing.

Michael And, anyway, you always get a pound for your birthday and can pay Aunty Mary back if you have to.

William That's right! You are an interesting boy. I was beginning to think you weren't worth bothering about, I must say, but you seem quite an interesting type. You are keen on sleeping out of doors with just a rug and some summer-house cushions, aren't you?

Michael Oh, yes.

William Gosh, you are all right then. What a scream you being Herbert!

Michael Most ingenious! Woof! Woof!

William It's all right, Herbert, you silly dog, it's only Roger coming back.

Roger enters

Roger Hello, you two. It's really most queer, and very puzzling!

William If there's a tale to tell, I think we'd better eat first!

Roger Good idea, William, I'm starving.

They make a dive for the basket, pull out serviettes, wipe their mouths and the meal is over

That was delicious.

Michael I've been thinking. I have an idea I know what that ticket is.

Roger Do tell, Herbert.

Michael It's a dry-cleaning ticket.

William You are a clever old dog, Herbert. But how did you know that?

Michael Well, one of our servants used to work for a dry cleaners, and he told me about the tickets. The perforation is where the ticket comes in half, so the customer keeps one half, and the other stays with the clothes so that they know whose is which.

Roger Amazing! I do believe you're right, Herbert, well done! So whoever dropped it must have taken something to the cleaners!

Michael Almost right, Roger. But the half we have is the half that stays with the clothes, so whoever dropped it must work for a dry-cleaning firm!

Roger How lucky we were to find you, Herbert! Even if you haven't got a sensitive nose, you can certainly sniff out the clues!

They all laugh

William But come on, Roger, we can wash up the plates and things in the stream later. I'm simply bursting to hear what you discovered!

Michael Yes, do tell!

Roger Well, when I'd poured in the plaster, here's the cast by the way (*he brings out the plaster cast from his pocket*), you can see the shoe belongs to someone pretty down-at-heel, I decided to follow the tracks. And here's the puzzling part; they led down to the school for the village children by the back way, right down to the headmaster's office window.

William Well, I'm blessed!—as my daddy might say.

Roger I looked in, but everything seemed in apple-pie order, the window hadn't been opened from the outside, there was still dust on the sill, and then the tracks led back up the path to the road. It's all most queer!

Michael It would have been queerer if they had led to a cave.

Roger I agree, but there's nothing we can do about that.

William Was there a safe in the headmaster's study?

Roger Why yes, I believe there was.

William Then I know what the numbers on the back of the ticket are: the combination of the safe!

Roger Whoever it was must have sneaked down to the window, waited till the headmaster opened the safe, made a note of the numbers, twelve right twenty-one left three right four left, then sneaked away again, and when he'd memorized the combination, thrown the ticket away.

Michael Someone's coat will go astray at the cleaners!

William Yes. They must be planning to come back and break in tonight when it's dark.

Roger But what for? The village school safe is hardly likely to be full of pound notes.

Michael I know what'd be in the safe!

William What?

Michael The eleven-plus papers!

Roger Gosh! Of course!

Michael Whoever it is is going to steal one of the papers and work out the answers so that their child will pass without doing any work, and go to a better school than they deserve!

William Cheating! That's terrible.

Roger What sort of a father must he be?

Michael Horrid! Well, what are we going to do about it?
Roger Wait till it's dark and then wait by the road and follow him down to the school and catch him in the act.
Michael What shall we do till it gets dark?
William I know. Go and swim in that lovely deserted rock pool. It's a jolly good job we brought our swimming things with us.

The Lights go down. They take torches from the basket and switch them on. An owl hoots

Roger There's something coming.
William It's a car!
Michael No. It's a dry-cleaning van.
Roger It's slowing down.
Michael It's stopped! Someone's getting out!
William He's going down the path to the school.
Roger Give him a few moments and we'll follow. (*He checks a footprint against the plaster cast*) Identical! It's him all right.

They follow cautiously. Glass crash

William That must be the window. He's breaking in. Now then, Herbert, you stand guard outside the window and don't let him out. We must go and warn the police. Come on, Roger. He should get a few years for this.
Roger And his miserable little boy.

Roger and William exit

George enters

Michael flashes his torch on him

Michael Dad! It's you!

Fantasy ends

George Michael, take that torch out of my eyes. What are you doing up here with the light off? (*He turns the lights on*) That's better. You coming down for your tea? Your mother's been calling you for the last half-hour.
Michael Yes, in a minute.
George Come on, son, it's pineapple chunks!

They exit

BLACK-OUT

ACT II

Scene 1

1957. The Arnold Riley Grammar School for Boys

Michael and Owen enter with ruler and textbook each. Owen reads upstage while Michael addresses the audience

Michael What schools do you lot go to, then? I go to the Arnold Riley Grammar School for Boys. I'm in the first form, 1A. Really, I wish you hadn't asked me that because it seems like I'm bragging which is something I can't stand. My mum and dad do it a lot. "Our Michael goes to Arnold Riley, you know, the grammar school", they keep on saying to everybody. My mum even tells strangers. It takes her on average twenty-five seconds from meeting someone for the first time to telling them that I go to the grammar school. The average would have been lower than that but last week she met a lady whose husband had just died and out of respect she left it a minute and a half. Do you have to wear your blazer when your aunts and uncles come round? I do. And she always finds an excuse to look round the garden so I can put my cap on. My blazer costs five pounds five and tuppence because it's pure worsted, W-O-R-S-T-E-D, unlike the town which is spelt . . . differently. They were going to get me the wool mixture at seventy-nine and eleven but that would have been false economy. They also got me a brief case which is better than a duffel bag for books but useless for games kit. So when we have games I put my shoes in the brief case and go home in my rugby boots. We've not only got to read all these books, I've also got to cover them in brown paper. So that we can hand them back in the same condition we received them. My mate, Owen, says the best way to stop them getting damaged is not to give them out in the first place. That way everyone would be saved a lot of trouble. Owen's all right, really. He wants to be a pilot. I wouldn't mind being a pilot, but what I'd really like to be is a missionary.

Scene 2

1958. Michael imagines himself a missionary saving black sinners, and enjoys the delicious pain of self-sacrifice

During Michael's first speech he pretends to write his missionary's journal in the textbook

Michael The fourth of May, eighteen hundred and ninety-three. Success at last! Today, at breakfast, I received news from Mr Owen in Bristol. A ship has been procured for the voyage to Africa. Now can I heed Christ's clarion call, "Go ye into the world and preach the Gospel to every creature". The Lord be praised. These glad tidings from Bristol have thrown the entire household into the most excited activity. Even my mother, so recently risen from her sickbed, has spent the whole day supervising the packing of my trunks.

Michael places the two chairs to create a ship and installs Owen as its helmsman

But what of the ship that will carry us to Africa just as the lowly ass bore Our Lord into Jerusalem? With his usual apprehensiveness, which, after the affairs at the inn, I have come now to view as most genuine concern for my safety, Mr Owen informs me in his letter that though the vessel is neither the greatest nor the soundest in God's Creation, yet might she serve, God willing, to bear us and our equipment to that heathen shore. How my heart soars! The weaker the vessel the greater glory to God. Weakness does not hinder. Lack of faith does. Well, Mr Owen, there, below the horizon, sinks fair Albion. What rises next is darkest Africa.

Owen Ay, sir, and black and heathen it will be, too. But not half as evil as the hearts of the men that loiter in the fo'c'sle now, sir, with but one word upon their lips.

Michael What word is that, Mr Owen?

Owen Why mutiny, Father Peters, mutiny!

Michael Can it be so? Do obedience, respect, love and loyalty fall off our ship, even as does England's coastline now?

Owen becomes Bos'n Owen, leader of the mutiny

Owen Ay, Father Peters, they do. And I've a list here as long as your arm of reasons why: namely, one: you don't let us imbibe no grog. And, two: . . . two: (*stepping out of character*) you're always putting your hand up first in class and asking for extra homework which really gets up my nose . . .

Michael Enough, Bos'n! Your own words condemn you. You're a lazy, mutinous crew that won't see further than the end of your own bowsprits. I go about my Heavenly Father's business. And so ought you. Let's not forget our mission to carry the Good Book to heathen shores. To bring Christ's glorious knowledge to the ignorant savages of Africa.

Owen Is that your final word, Father Peters? You won't meet our demands?

Michael No, I'll meet 'em, Bos'n, with a sword!

The Boys fight with rulers. Owen wins. But Michael ignores this and kills Owen to be able to get on with his story

The fourth of May, eighteen hundred and ninety-four. One whole year has passed since we began our journey and, oh, how this fever grips me!

Owen grips Michael, attempting to add to the improvisation

Without the Lord's mercy and Owen, my faithful black servant,

Owen now reluctantly becomes the black servant

my race would long since have ended. Of our original party there is now but left two of us. Those that, by God's grace, survived the mutiny, the attacks by pirates, the water spout and the shipwreck upon the sea, have long since perished here upon the land. For the heat, the disease, the wild beasts and even wilder savages contrive to make the African jungle the vilest hell on earth. But in the deeper pit, there loudest cry sweet Jesu's name. And the darker the night the brighter the candle. We must not forget our mission. The Lord's name shall be held on high even here in Africa.

Owen Father Peters, Massa.

Michael Yes, Owen, my faithful black servant?

Owen De big chief of de tribe him dying. Him got one foot in de grave. Big chief, him say white massa got big magic. Him say white massa make big chief well.

Michael Not I, Owen, but the Lord.

Owen White massa make big chief well, big chief make white massa big chief's son-in-law.

Michael We labour and ask for no reward save that of knowing that we do His will.

Michael pounds his chair to emphasize these last three words and Owen takes this as his cue to begin beating the drums on the other chair

But why sound the drum, Owen?

Owen Big chief also say, on de other hand, white massa not make big chief shipshape and Bristol fashion, big chief's folks make white massa and white massa's faithful black servant, yours truly, very dead, Boss.

Michael Then let us take the Good Book and place the big chief's hand upon it. What evil vapours shall withstand such medicine? Oh God, in whose name we trust, look down on this black and savage sinner and have mercy upon him.

After a lengthy drum solo Owen condescends to stop

But why stop the drums, Owen?

Owen Lordy, lordy, we hab missed de boat dis time, Massa. Big chief him gone and snuffed it.

During the following speech Owen, again reluctantly, does what Michael tells him

Michael Then stand by me, Owen, for now must we surely perish. The fourth of May, in the year of Our Lord, eighteen hundred and ninety-five, upon which day, exactly two years since, we began this our joyous crusade. Today the drums stopped beating. For the Lord, in his infinite wisdom, has seen fit to take Onwabi, Chief of the Sintu, unto Himself. And thus we stood, myself a child of God, and Owen, my faithful black helpmate in Christ, before the slowly advancing tribesmen. Naked they were, and devilishly painted, bearing nought before them save their pipes, from which would shoot at some unseen command, their venomous darts. Unseen? Yea, to my eyes, but not so to Owen's. For as the first deadly dart sped towards my unprotected breast, that good soul threw himself before me, took the poisonous tip within his own heart, and dying fell. True friend, black body bleeding with blood as red as any fair-skinned Christian man's, how noble was thy sacrifice. And yet in vain! For following came the deluge. Dart after dart pierced my body. With every breath I breathed my breast heaved up a hundred quills. Dug deep with dead and dying, yet lived I still. (*He dies. Then comes back to life to continue the saga. Ecstatic groans*) And still I lived . . .

An electric school bell cuts him short and they go off to their lessons

Scene 3

1961. "Don't lark about with a girl whom you would not like your mother or sister to see you with. Don't make love to any girl unless you mean to marry her."—Baden Powell, Scouting for Boys

Michael enters as a boy scout. He presses the bell on an automatic door opener

Lady (*off, entryphone effect*) Hello.
Michael Good-morning, madam. I'm Patrol Leader Michael Peters. I'm from the Fifth Bellevue Troop. I don't know if you're aware of the fact but it's Bob-a-job week. Would you care to support the scouting movement?
Lady (*off*) I'd like to try. What can you do?
Michael Cut logs, make camp beds, stalk game, read signs, estimate the distance across a river, throw a rope bridge over a ravine, send messages in semaphore, dig latrines, and bake hedghogs in clay.
Lady (*off*) Goodness, you sound like a one man Jamboree. Are you a big scout or a little scout?
Michael I'm not a Wolf Cub, madam, I'm a senior scout.
Lady (*off*) Top flat, come up.

Buzz of the door being opened automatically

Michael exits

The Lady enters

Michael enters

Lady What a big boy!
Michael Yes.
Lady And what a lot of badges! What's that one for?
Michael It means I'm First Class.
Lady Are you? It's very pretty.
Michael Thank you. The design also serves to remind the scout of some of the more important aspects of scouting. It depicts an arrowhead because

a scout points out the path to follow. The arrow is in three parts because there are three parts to the scout promise. The knot is to remind him to do a good turn for someone every day. And the scroll is our motto, "Be Prepared". It's turned up at the ends like that to represent a scout's mouth. He smiles cheerfully through everything.

Lady How fascinating.

Michael And whistles when in difficulty.

Lady Would you like a drink?

Michael Scouts aren't meant to drink.

Lady I shan't tell.

Michael Perhaps I could have a lemonade or something after the job.

Lady Now how much is a very experienced, first-class young man going to cost me?

Michael Well, it's up to you; however much you can spare. A shilling is the minimum.

Lady Oh, more than a shilling, surely.

Michael I'd rather do it for nothing, that'd be best. What is the job madam?

Lady What are you good at?

Michael Semaphore.

Lady Are you trying to tell me your interest is flagging? What are all these?

Michael This one's for pioneering. This one's for camp cooking. This one's for first aid.

Lady That's it. That's what I want.

Michael Lie down. Why didn't you say sooner?

The Lady lies prone

Lady I've only just seen the possibilities.

Michael Now what is it? Grit in the eye, snake bite, fits, fish hook in the skin, hysterics . . . ?

Lady Hysterics?

Michael Yes, nervous people, especially women, get hysterics. The best treatment is to shut the patient into a room and leave him entirely alone till he gets over it.

Lady It's my back.

Michael I'd better call an ambulance.

Lady No, there's no need for that. I think you can manage it.

Michael What is it then?

Lady I like having it rubbed.

Michael starts to whistle "We're Riding Along On The Crest Of A Wave" etc.

Come along. A scout's duty is to be useful and to help others. I really need a hand, firmly between my shoulder blades.

Michael I'm sorry. I'm not prepared to . . .

Lady You must Be Prepared to . . . between my shoulder blades.

Michael tentatively massages her back

That's it. And up and down my spine. Yes, that's it. What strong hands you've got. Is that from swinging axes?

Michael I expect so. There, that should have done the trick. If you'd like to sign my card I'll be on my way.
Lady Don't stop. It's just beginning to work.

Michael continues

Do you like being a scout?
Michael Yes. No. It has its moments.
Lady I'm sure it does.
Michael Camping for instance.
Lady Good, clean fun, eh?
Michael Yes, that's it.
Lady But a bit dull surely?
Michael (*sitting astride her and massaging with his hands*) No, not when you get into it.
Lady What about girls, though?
Michael What about them?
Lady I mean they don't camp with you, do they? They have a different movement.
Michael Yes, that's because they have larger pelvic girdles.

She turns over beneath him

Lady Do they? Tell me about it.
Michael I didn't mean to say that.
Lady Why have you got your eyes closed?
Michael I'm practising Kim's game. I'm trying to remember how many objects are in front of me. Have you had enough?
Lady Have you?
Michael Is your back better?
Lady I don't think you've finished yet.
Michael Well I can't do much if you're lying on it.
Lady (*raising herself towards him*) Do what you can, then.

Michael feels his hands drawn to her breasts

That's better.
Michael I don't think this is right.
Lady It's not. You're not moving your hands. Is it such a traumatic experience?
Michael No.
Lady Have you already done your good deed for the day?
Michael You can do as many as you like.
Lady What's the matter, then?
Michael Well, a scout is clean in thought, word and deed. That is, he looks down upon a silly youth who talks dirt, and he does not himself give way to temptation, either to talk it or think or do anything dirty. A scout is clean-minded and manly.
Lady Both at the same time? It sounds like a contradiction.
Michael It is, but I've only just seen why. Can I come back when I'm a Rover?

Michael and the Lady exit

Scene 4

1961. "The Art of Conversation" is brought home by Michael from the grammar school. Its chances of survival are slim

George and Enid enter to watch TV. Michael enters and turns it off

George 'Ere! What do you think you're doing?
Enid Turn it on again, Michael. We're watching that.
Michael It's only commercials.
George Yes, but there's something else on in a minute.
Michael What is it?
George I don't know. Something your mum wants, I expect.
Enid I don't know. Switch it on. It might be good.
Michael Then you weren't really looking forward to it.
George What's going on, Michael?
Michael I want to talk to you.
George Well, you could have just turned the sound down.
Michael Please.
George All right then. Yes. All right.
Michael So can we just talk?
George Yes, that's a good idea, Michael. We are a family, after all. What do you want to say then?
Michael I don't want to say anything.
George I thought you wanted to talk to us?
Michael No, I want you to talk to me. Or just talk to each other and I'll listen. If something interesting comes up, I'll join in.
George I see. Is it a game?
Michael No.
Enid What do you want us to talk about then?
Michael Anything. Anything you've noticed or found interesting or want to do.
Enid You start then, George.
George Er. Did I ever tell you about my friend Dan?
Enid Yes. But Michael hasn't heard it.
Michael Yes, I have. But it doesn't matter. Tell me again.
George There's no point in me telling you again, is there? Not if you've heard it before. Your turn then, Enid.
Michael It doesn't have to be in turns! You just talk, naturally.
George Well, you're the one who's got the interesting life, Michael. We're quite happy to listen to you.
Michael I could talk all evening, but you wouldn't be able to join in. You'll have to start.
George My mind's gone blank. What's all this about, Michael?
Michael Nothing.
George Yes, it is.
Michael Well, suppose I had to write an essay on "A Typical Evening at Home".

George Have you?
Michael No. But it would be dead easy, wouldn't it? One word: Nothing.
Enid They wouldn't give you such a difficult subject.
Michael It's not a difficult subject. It should be rich and funny and exciting.
George You could make it up.
Michael No, I'd want it to be real. Everyone else's would be real.
Enid You could describe the front room now your dad's decorated it. I'll put the kettle on.

Enid exits

Michael That's about it, isn't it? The sum total of your existence: you decorate the front room, watch television in it, have six pots of tea, and then retire exhausted to bed!
George Don't get sarky, Michael. We don't go making sarky comments about you, do we? I'm tired when I come home from work.
Michael Yes, I know, but you could do something. Why don't you have someone round?
George: We're not that sort of person.

Michael exits

I see other people all day at work. We don't need other people to enjoy ourselves of an evening. We're a family.

George exits

Scene 5

1963. Michael Peters, seeing himself as James Bond, takes on "The Head" and gives the French Assistante more than she bargained for

Mademoiselle and Michael enter

Mademoiselle Bonjour, Michel. Comment ça va?
Michael Assez bien, merci, Mademoiselle Leblanc. Et vous?
Mademoiselle Comme ci, comme ça. Vous êtes seul aujourd'hui?
Michael Oui. Je crois que les autres sont absents.
Mademoiselle Eh, bien, la conversation française entre nous deux. Qu'est-ce que vous avez fait cette semaine?
Michael Presque rien, comme d'habitude: les leçons, les devoirs, rien de plus.
Mademoiselle Mais pensez. Nous devons parler. Qu'est ce que vous pensez des lycéens anglais comme vous?
Michael Er er, je crois que, je ne suis pas certain de—répétez vous, s'il vous plaît.
Mademoiselle Oh Peters! Every week we go through this charade of French conversation. You always tell me you have done nothing, you are just a schoolboy, so we talk of autumn, pieces of theatre, la vie française.

Fantasy begins and Michael becomes James Bond for the rest of the scene

Let us be frank. You are not Michael Peters, and I am not Françoise Leblanc. We both know why we are here, and time is getting short. You can trust me, James Bond double-o-seven of Her Majesty's Secret Service!

Michael Incroyable! What makes you think I am not Michael Peters?

Mademoiselle One or two little things I have noticed. First, there is your physique: superb. Second, under that ridiculous English schoolboy blazer you wear a handmade sea island cotton shirt with your black silk knitted tie. Then you do not take school dinners.

Michael Many of the boys bring a packed lunch.

Mademoiselle Underdone tournedos à la sauce Béarnaise with coeur d'artichaut and a bottle of Tattainger Blanc de Brut 'forty-three?

Michael So I like good food and drink.

Mademoiselle You overtook the one-eight-three bus this morning on your way to school in a nineteen thirty four-and-a-half-litre supercharged Bentley.

Michael I thought the L plates would fool you.

Mademoiselle You were wearing your Arnold Riley cap, Bond.

Michael What are you going to do then, keep me in after school?

Mademoiselle Don't think it hasn't crossed my mind, James. I am your French contact, Ophelia Plenty.

Michael All in good time. (*Aside*) Something about the jutting swell of her pointed hillocks, her square-toed shoes, and the thick weight of hair at the nape of the neck told me she was no ordinary French Assistante. How did you get into the Service?

Mademoiselle My father was a great chef, pressed into service by the Nazis during the occupation, but he passed on information to the Resistance. When the Gestapo shot him, my mother, my brothers and sisters, I alone escaped, and vowed to fight always for freedom.

Michael Good girl. Did your father serve rognon de veau with pommes sautés followed by fraises des bois?

Mademoiselle Of course. Oh James, it has been an agony, waiting till I could reveal myself. I want you, James. I want you to do everything to me. Everything you've ever done to a woman. Now, please.

Michael Certainly, chou-fleure. What have you been able to find out?

Mademoiselle Someone in the school is attempting to brainwash the sixth form.

Michael Right. The boys have been implanted with something which makes them completely servile. It's pathetic: instead of living the life of red-blooded young males, they stay in at night doing homework, they do virtually without money and sex, display amazing anxiety over exams, and are prepared to bully younger boys of their own class in an obsequious desire to please masters. But who is behind it all?

Mademoiselle One of the arch fiends of all time. He's subtle, ruthless, mad, and physically revolting. So important is he in the underworld, they call him The Head.

Michael The Head! Of course, his earlobes are too long, and his fat lips always wet. But what is his aim?

Mademoiselle He wants to rule the world through these automatons, and he holds sway over them with a terrible promise: success. Success that is always just another exam away. Careful, James. The skeleton butt of your point two-five Beretta is interfering with the mysterious promise of my folded thighs.

Michael We must liquidate him.

Mademoiselle You do it, James. I can watch. When this is all over, we could get married. You do love me just a little, don't you, James?

Michael Thanks for telling me what you know, Miss Plentsky.

Mademoiselle James!

Michael You bitch! You're a double agent. You're SMERSH.

Mademoiselle Oh, James, I feel so guilty. How did you know?

Michael Rognon de veau is served with pommes soufflés, not sautés.

Mademoiselle But they forced me, James. I love you.

Michael You would have used me to get rid of The Head, then killed me and used his secrets to control innocent schoolboys in Georgia for your own vile communistic ends!

Mademoiselle Oh, it's true! It's true!

The Head enters. He holds a cane

The Head I congratulate you, Mr Bond. A remarkable piece of deduction. Such a pity it should come to nothing.

Mademoiselle
Michael } (*together*) The Head!

The Head I have heard everything, my dear boy. How clever of my old school chum M to infiltrate double o-seven as a schoolboy. But for Ophelia Plentsky, your cover would remain intact, so I think it only fair that she should die first and leave us boys together, don't you? (*He stabs her with the end of the cane*)

She dies slowly

Michael You swine!

The Head Come, Mr Bond, she is our mutual enemy.

Michael But she is a beautiful woman!

The Head How touching and quaint that you should fall victim to the weakness of flesh we call lust. You should know never to trust a woman, James. Now she's quiet, we can enjoy ourselves. No heroics please. (*He rips open Michael's shirt, draws blood with the cane*) What fine red blood you have, James. You will write me a thousand lines in it before you die.

Michael You're mad, The Head!

The Head Tush, I think "I must not be a secret agent in class" would be appropriate, don't you?

Michael What do you hope to gain with this scheme of yours?

The Head Do not play the dull and stupid schoolboy, James. You know you are capable of much better work. I already control the most intelligent young men in England. What is to stop me taking over the world?

Michael Damn the Welfare State!

The Head Quite. I think perhaps I should cane you to death, no? Drop your trousers. Bend over. (*He is paralysed as he draws his arm back*) Aagh! But what is happening to me?

Michael You underestimated me, The Head. As I dropped my trousers, I released a tiny spider stolen from the biology lab. It has bitten your jugular.

The Head Poisonous insects in the school? The PTA wouldn't allow it!

Michael On its own the spider is quite harmless. But the catalyst with which I spiked the staffroom tea makes the venom deadly. I'll take that. (*He seizes the Head's cane*)

The Head Finish with me, I beg you.

Michael Not after the way you dealt with Ophelia. Your agony will be overwhelming. You have just a few minutes, the only part of your body not paralysed is the larynx. Now talk.

Michael exits with Ophelia's corpse

SCENE 6

1964. Speech Day

The Head unfreezes and addresses the audience

The Head Well, the Hutchinson Prize for Expertise in Biology Practical—well done again, Owen—brings us to the end of the main part of Prize Giving and leaves only our most coveted award, The Arnold Riley Prize itself, which goes to Michael Peters of the Upper Sixth Arts. And I hope I shan't embarrass Michael too much by saying that the committee meeting to decide who should receive this award was one of the shortest I have had the pleasure of chairing. I know I can rest assured that when, sadly, Michael leaves us at the end of term, becomes an Old Boy of the school, an Old Arnold Rileyonian, and goes on to higher things at the University, he will go forth armed with this book as our ambassador, representing all our hopes and ideals, symbolized completely in the name Arnold Riley. Come along, Michael.

He beckons an imaginary Michael from the audience, then turns to meet Michael for Scene 7

SCENE 7

18th July 1964. For the Arnold Riley prize-winner, honesty is the best policy. But the Arnold Riley prize-giver finds the truth inconvenient

Michael enters

The Head Sit down. Would you like a sherry? I suppose you've been round the farewell route of the rest of the staff?

Michael Yes, sir. Before break.

The Head Good. I'm sorry all this had to happen on your last day, Michael. A few irresponsibles doing their level best to muck it up for the leavers.

Michael Sir?

The Head I mean this hymn book business. What kind of mentality do some of these boys have, Michael? God, there are bleak moments in this job you know. High spirits on the last day at school, that's traditional. The Feast of Fools. It does one good to have one's dignity pricked occasionally, but this is something quite different: sheer, wanton destruction. Anyway, it's got nothing to do with you. When do you go up?

Michael It was my idea, sir, the hymn books.

The Head Your idea?

Michael Yes, sir.

The Head I see. You've grown out of that schoolboy honour, surely?

Michael Pardon?

The Head I know when someone's covering up for someone else.

Michael I'm not covering up for someone else, sir. It was my idea to take everyone's hymn book: so they couldn't sing "Lord dismiss us with thy blessing" this afternoon. I thought it would be a good joke.

The Head A joke? I'm afraid you don't know the full circumstances of what has happened, Michael. Now don't be foolish, not now. The sherry hasn't gone to your head, has it?

Michael No, sir. But I did take the hymn books.

The Head For goodness' sake! You're the Arnold Riley prize-winner! Don't tell me you feel nothing for this place, you've helped make the school what it is! You're covering up for someone!

Michael I'm not, sir. It was me. I thought it would be the best rag stunt yet: a harmless embarrassment.

The Head You're being embarrassing now. Please don't persist, you're making a fool of yourself and that's not like you. I don't like it. You're not capable of this. You're an intelligent young man.

Michael Yes, I am intelligent, I am young, I may be making a fool of myself, but I am quite capable of thinking up a stunt like that. I know because I did it. It would have been hilarious if it had come off. Everyone knows the religious assemblies are a joke. You only have them because you have to. Oh come on, sir. You're always telling us you were young once. You've got to admit it's funny!

The Head Did you really do it?

Michael Yes, and I'm afraid I don't even regret it. I may be a prefect, and I'm not unfond of the school, but I'm also a human being, not some paragon of virtue walking in the footsteps of Arnold Riley.

The Head Michael!

Michael But since you landed me with that ticket, I think you might have the decency to believe me when I tell you it was me, sir.

The Head In the seventeen years I've been Headmaster of this school I've never been spoken to like that, not by anyone. I believe you *are* responsible!

Michael Yes, sir, I am.

The Head And you're brazen with it. I see a lot of things now. You've been making a mockery of the trust I placed in you for years. Easy target, am I? What do you do? Make snide remarks about an institution your gutter mentality can't even begin to match up to? And all the time deceive your betters with that smug "yes sir" face and your glittering exam results? You mean, ungrateful, two-faced rat! It was you who stole the fifth-form ballroom dancing records, wasn't it?

Michael No! Calm down, sir.

The Head And I blamed the cleaners! Don't you lie to me now, boy. If you're low enough to burn six hundred hymn books, you're low enough for anything.

Michael Burn them?

The Head You know what I'm talking about. Don't try and worm your way out now!

Michael What makes you think I was going to burn them?

The Head They were stuffed in the stoves of the overspill huts. Why are you laughing? How dare you laugh?

Michael I wasn't going to burn them. I was just hiding them in there.

The Head You were going to burn them, foiled however by Mr Jones finding them first.

Michael Where would you hide six hundred hymn books in the summer term? The heating stoves were the only place. The last place you'd look. Why should I want to burn them?

The Head You don't honestly expect me to believe that now. I've found out just what you are.

Michael You're wrong!

The Head Don't worry. You'll get away with it this time. I shall have to cover up. Your name's on the Honours Board. Not to save your worthless hide, but to prevent a smear on the name of Arnold Riley!

Michael And I stole the fifth-form dance records? You called me two-faced a moment ago. I'd like to return the compliment. I should have got into trouble more often. It's quite an eye opener. Well at least now I can see. You. You're blind. I wish I had been going to burn them.

Michael exits

The Head Come back here! Peters! Peters!

The Head exits

Scene 8

18th July 1964. Michael's untried theory, that anyone who is prepared to make the necessary effort can succeed in life, doesn't correspond with George's lifetime's experience

George enters smoking a cigarette, followed by Michael

Michael What's the matter?
George I'm all right.
Michael Why aren't you at work?
George I didn't feel too grand. I've got a bit of a chest.
Michael Too many cigarettes.
George You sound like your mother. Anyway, these small ones aren't as bad. They don't last as long.
Michael You just smoke more of them.
George I've only had three today.
Michael It's your life.
George There's some tea in the pot. I've only just made it.
Michael Have you had anything to eat?
George I've had a sandwich. I'm all right. You have something if you want though.
Michael I had dinner at school.
George You'll be leaving there soon, won't you?
Michael I left today.
George I thought you weren't leaving till the eighteenth.
Michael It's the eighteenth today.
George Is it? Are you sure? Where's a paper? That'll tell us.
Michael It's the eighteenth.
George I don't know, this month's flying by. Time seems to go so much faster nowadays, Michael. It'll soon be Christmas at this rate. I don't suppose it can go quick enough for you, eh, son? Are you looking forward to going?
Michael I'm not sure I am yet, am I?
George Don't say that.
Michael I don't know for certain, do I?
George When do you get your results?
Michael August.
George You'll be all right. You've done all right up to now.
Michael Have to see, won't we?
George I'd put money on it, Michael. I've always known you had it in you. Even when you were a little kid, I could tell. You had an inquiring mind. Your mother used to say, "Look at him, George, playing with his toys, building them up, he looks just like you!" Even now you remind her of how I used to look when I was younger. No, but you won't be like me. You won't have to go through all what I've had to. You'll do fine, Michael. You'll be able to go in at the top. Not fiddle around for years like I've had to. I don't know, you'd think it'd get easier as you got older wouldn't you? But even with this job I'm in now they still take liberties with you. They're forever finding ways they can give you less or make you do twice as much.
Michael You want to do something about it.
George What can you do?

Michael Chuck it in! If you don't like the way you're being treated at work, change your job.

George Not when you're my age. Not everyone wants to take on a bloke my age.

Michael Anyone'd think you were an old man of ninety the way you go on! How old are you? Fifty-odd. Churchill was sixty-four when the war started. Dad, it's an attitude of mind. DO something about it or stop moaning.

George You don't understand.

Michael What don't I understand? Come on! Tell me!

George Firms aren't interested in someone my age when they can get a young bloke.

Michael You've put your finger on it there! They're not *interested* because you're not *interesting*. In fact, you're bloody boring.

George Thank you very much. And I suppose you're awfully fascinating?

Michael Yes, I am, compared to you.

George Because we've seen to it that you've had a decent education.

Michael Well, why don't you do the same for yourself? There are all sorts of libraries and evening classes if only you could be bothered to join.

George It's hard when you're my age.

Michael Here we go again. I reckon you were born fifty.

George Sometimes you're typical of the worst elements. I suppose that's what they teach you at that school: how to cheek your olders! Well, I could still put you over my knee, young man!

Michael That'd solve everything, wouldn't it?

George It'd knock a bit of sense into you, I know that!

Michael How do you always manage to turn a sensible discussion into a heated argument?

George Because you're such a bleeding big head, that's why! What do you know about going to work?

Michael Very little!

George You know nothing!

Michael And what do you know?

George I know it's a lot harder than you imagine!

Michael Do you know what your trouble is? You're afraid! Afraid to stand up for yourself. Afraid to take what you want! Because most of all you're just dead.

Michael exits, then George

Scene 9

1966. Paint on a wall or paint on a person but not at the same time. Michael has a lot to learn

Michael and Girl Friend enter with brushes and buckets

Girl Friend What's so special about this wall, Mike?

Michael This is the American Tourist Office. Everyone'll be able to see it here. Put that spare bucket out of sight in the alley.

She puts her bucket offstage

Now, you know what to do, don't you? You start at that end with "Victory to the NLF" and I'll get on with "Death to US Imperialism" at this end. Then we can do "Yanks out of Vietnam" together. OK?

Girl Friend Mike, I love you.
Michael Great.
Girl Friend Give us a kiss.

They kiss

Michael Don't use all the paint. I want to do the ceiling in our kitchen when we've finished, all right?

They begin painting. The paint is mimed. There is singing, off

Girl Friend Mike!
Michael What?
Girl Friend Someone's coming.
Michael Fuzz?
Girl Friend No. It's someone on his own.
Michael Stay in the shadow.

Offstage crash of foot in bucket

Girl Friend He's fallen over the bucket!
Irishman (*off*) Jesus, Mary and Joseph!

Irishman enters with the lower left leg covered in wet paint. (It's not necessary to actually use wet paint. Some repeatable "cod" effect is required: e.g. a white shoe, white sock, and white turn-up on trouser leg.) He sings "We're all off to Dublin in the Green"

Michael Please be quiet.
Irishman Oh, I'm sorry, sir. Is it a hospital?
Michael No, it's the American Tourist Office. Now be quiet, please. We're working.
Irishman Work's a wonderful thing . . . when you can get it. I wonder, sir, could you perhaps spare me, you know, just for a cup of tea and a bite, I haven't eaten . . . Ah! Good-evening, miss. I'm sorry to be holding up the work.
Michael We haven't got anything.
Girl Friend We're students from the University.
Irishman God, they work you all hours.
Michael No. This isn't college work.
Irishman You're working nights, to make up the grant? Oh, that's terrible, terrible. It's the Government. I don't know why you don't have the demonstration about it. I can get you the guns.
Michael We're painting the wall with anti-American slogans: "Victory to the NLF", "Death to US Imperialism", "Yanks out of Vietnam".

Irishman Don't you like the Americans?

Michael They're murdering innocent people in South-East Asia.

Irishman Who is it?

Michael Johnson.

Irishman I give up with some people. What's he want to do that for then, the murdering swine?

Girl Friend He's denying the right of the Vietnamese people to decide their own future because what they want conflicts with American financial interests.

Michael He's trying to push people around.

Irishman Right, lads, I'm with you. Give me a brush.

Michael We've only got the two.

Irishman Then step down for a minute, sir, and lend me yours. I'll give the lady a hand.

Girl Friend Go on, Mike. Give him the brush.

Michael He wouldn't know what to write. Anyway, he's pissed.

Girl Friend Go on. It's you that's always saying people are never given the chance to express themselves.

Michael This is serious.

Girl Friend Don't be so pompous.

Michael offers the brush to the Irishman

Michael You know what you're going to write?

Irishman Oh, yes. (*He paints*)

Michael (*reading*) "Up the IRA". I told you! That's not what we agreed on. Give me the brush.

Irishman Sure, it's the same thing. It's us versus them. (*He turns back to the wall and becomes aware of his white leg*) Oh, he's a comical bloke. We have a slight ideological confliction, and your man here pours paint down my leg! Up the Republic!

He dabs Michael's nose with the brush. The Girl Friend laughs. Michael takes the brush and dabs the Girl Friend. She dabs him back and Michael retaliates. They see the funny side of this and cover one another in paint. The sequence ends with the Girl Friend putting the upturned bucket over Michael's head. The Irishman becomes the Magistrate

The Girl Friend exits

Magistrate Michael Peters, according to the uncontested account of your activities last night given in evidence by PC Grahame, you seem to be an extremely confused young man. You are not unintelligent, but your squalid behaviour, defacing private property with mindless slogans, bringing your girl friend, Miss Smith, into conflict with the law, and your association with common vagrants speaks more of the gutter than the institution of learning of which you are an undergraduate. You have brought nothing but shame upon your university, your school and your parents. In extenuation I have nothing to consider but that this is your first conviction and your youth, though at twenty most young men seem to have found a more responsible attitude to their fellows. May I suggest you sit down and have a long hard think about your future? Do you intend to take advantage of the privileged opportunities society has seen fit to offer you, or will your behaviour give the Law and your Vice-Chancellor no alternative but to send you down in disgrace at some future date? Have you anything to say?

Michael (*still with the bucket over his head*) What I wrote was not mindless.

Magistrate Fined fifteen pounds plus costs.

Michael and the Magistrate exit

Scene 10

1966. New Year's Eve. Michael's parents know something's gone wrong and Enid tries to define it

George and Enid enter

Enid I think I'll go to bed, George.

George No, don't do that, see the New Year in.

Enid I'm tired.

George Come on. It's not long now.

Enid I'm not bothered really.

George You a bit low? Have a drink. Let's both have a drink. Just the two of us. Shall we? Yes! (*He gives her a drink*) Get that down you. Here's to us in nineteen sixty-seven.

Enid Here's to us.

George Don't it sound queer, 'sixty-seven? Every New Year's strange at first. Cheer up. It might never happen. Don't you feel well?

Enid I told you, I'm tired.

George Well, we'll only hear Big Ben. Then we'll go to bed. We can't not see the New Year in, can we?

Enid I wonder what Michael's doing.

George You're not drinking.

Enid I wonder what he's doing, George.

George Don't you like it? I think this sherry of mine's turned out rather well.

Enid Why didn't he come home this Christmas?

George Enid, you said you wouldn't go on any more about it.

Enid I'm not going on about it. But I can't stop myself thinking.

George I suppose he wanted to be with his friends.

Enid Aren't we his friends?

George 'Course we're his friends.

Enid He wanted to be with that girl! That's why he didn't come home.

George It's only natural with someone his age.

Enid Not at Christmas. What if she had a baby? I wouldn't have minded if he'd brought her here even. Did you ever talk to him?

George Michael knows what he's doing. And if he doesn't, there's nothing we can do now. It's his life.

Enid Don't you miss him?

George You know I do.

Enid I miss him.

George We both do.

Enid Sometimes I wonder if we did the right thing, making him go to that school. Sometimes I think he might have been happier doing something else. I feel he hardly knows us now.

George We didn't make him. We tried to help him. Anyway, he didn't have to go. He wanted to.

Enid What about this girl? What about this going to court? What about the way he looks? And what he says?

George He's only doing what his own click does. That's what people are like.

Enid They don't all get involved with the police. Some of them have got more sense.

George I'll put the telly on. See what old Andy Stewart is doing up the White Heather Club. Shall we have another?

Enid No, I don't want any more. And I don't want the television on. And I don't want to go on pretending everything's all right when it's not. I want you to tell me what's happening. George, answer!

George I don't know what you want to know. Michael's got his own life to lead. He'll be all right.

Enid I'm not talking about Michael. I want to know about us.

George What about us?

Enid What's going to happen to us?

George When?

Enid When we die.

George Enid! I've let you go on and on but I can't take any more of this. You go from one thing to another, anything that comes into your head. You're not talking sense. What do you mean, "when we die"?

Enid I don't know. I've always thought we'd have Michael and now he's gone.

George Hang on. I think that's it. I can hear next-door's television. Happy New Year. (*He kisses her*)

George and Enid exit

Scene 11

1967. Michael finds that like the pound his degree has been devalued

A Doorman enters. Michael enters, carrying a briefcase, and approaches the five glass doors (mimed) of an office block. He tries each locked door in turn before gaining admittance by the door nearest the Doorman, who is inside the building

Doorman We're equalizing out the wear on the doors. We have a different one open depending what day it is. See, you went for the Monday door and today's a Friday. In fact, you trying to get in has given me a mental vista of my whole week.

Michael Why don't you let people use which door they want? They wouldn't all use the same one.

Doorman You don't know the people that work here. Nine-thirty of a morning they all used to pour through that end one. That was the only one they'd use. Because they worked out it was the nearest where they all wanted to get to, the lift, the cunning buggers! With never a thought for the trough they were going to wear in the pre-stressed reinforced concrete flooring. That's the type of thoughtless person I have to work with!

Michael Perhaps you should have explained to them the consequences of constantly using the same door.

Doorman I tried to, mate. I even made up a little notice: "DON'T ALWAYS USE THIS DOOR". But being reasonable gets you nowhere nowadays. They think you've gone soft. You should have seen them on the first morning I locked it. You'd see one of 'em come running up shouting to his friend, "See you at half-five, Nigel, for a game of squash", then thump against the plate glass'd go his nose. I shall never forget how their faces looked squashed up just for a moment like Cassius Clay had bopped 'em one. I even had one fella with a nose bleed. Now, how can I help you?

Michael I should like to see the Editor, please.

Doorman Have you got an appointment?

Michael No, but I think he'll be quite interested to meet me. You see, I've got an Honours Degree in English.

Doorman You should have rung up. We'd have sent a car round. Hop it!

Michael I don't think you quite understand. I'm a graduate and I've decided to be a journalist.

Doorman Deciding's one thing. Have you got the talent?

Michael Yes, I think so.

Doorman Aren't you sure?

Michael Of course I'm sure.

Doorman That's better, what experience have you had?

Michael My lack of professional experience is a positive advantage because I've got something to say and no hang-ups to prevent me saying it.

Doorman That don't make sense.

Michael Great minds think unalike.

Doorman I can't let you in without an appointment. Go home and write a letter.

Michael I've written twice. Both times I've got the same duplicated reply, "There is no suitable vacancy available at the moment". Anyway, that's the long way round. The mark of the educated man is his ability to find the short cut.

The Doorman decides to physically eject Michael and takes him by the scruff of the neck

Doorman Yes, but when too many people use the short cut you have to lock it.

Michael I'm one of the educational élite!

Doorman There's hundreds like you trying to get into this game, all got your degrees. What makes you better than the rest of them? I've got a lad like you. He's got a BA after his name. He's ambitious, but he's sensible. He's a personnel manager with Sainsbury's. (*Having continued to hold Michael by the scruff of the neck, he now drops him into a chair*)

The Doorman exits

SCENE 12

1968. Michael meets the Famous Five a second time. Their enemies are still not his enemies

Fantasy begins

Roger and William enter

Roger Hello, Herbert, you old dog. Long time no see.

William Hello Herbert! Gosh, how you've grown!

Roger We've come to offer our congratulations, old chap!

Michael Congratulations? What for?

Roger What a modest old hound he is, William

William Come on, Herbert, there's no use pretending. Everyone's heard about it—Sam the fisherman, the headmaster at the village school, even the local constable—and they all send you their congratulations.

Roger Yes, and hearty ones at that too. We all think it's a splendid appointment.

William Personnel Manager, Herbert!

Roger Top notch, old chap!

William Well done.

Michael I'd no idea you worked for this company too.

William Don't be a silly old dog, Herbert—we own it!

She slaps Michael on the back and Michael assumes the "Herbert the Dog" position on all fours

Roger Aunt Mary left it to us in her will so we're pretty much the major shareholders. Now here's the problem. Recently some nasty sort put up the cost of our raw materials.

William I said, "Let's put up our prices too".

Roger But if our goods become more expensive than the similar products of our rivals, our sales drop and down go the profits.

William Which would be horrid!

Roger So we have to find some other way to offset increased costs. Any bright ideas, Herbert?

Michael Reduce the wages bill.
Roger You mean pay the men less?
William Industrial suicide!
Roger Quite right, William.
Michael Reduce the work force, then.
Roger Lay some men off? That's better.
Michael Which ones, though?
William Leave that to us.
Roger We'll decide who's to go. All you have to do is tell them they're going.

Roger and William exit and enter immediately with George tied up in a sack

William Right-o Herbert, here's number one.
Roger Off you go, old chap. Do your stuff!
Michael (*to the sack*) In accordance with the agreed policy of periodic review with regard to the continued employment of manual staff at or near retirement age—Notice seven-three, stroke, four-one-nine—I have to inform you that your present employment with this company will be terminated with the completion of your duties for the fourth of March. This decision is covered by the Redundancy Payments Act.

Applause from Roger and William

Roger Lovely! Next one please, William.

Roger opens the sack, revealing George

Michael But this is my father!
William Is it?
Roger Never mind, Herbert, most of the men we employ are somebody's father.
Michael No, you don't understand. This is my father. He doesn't even work for this company.
William Don't be a silly old dog, Herbert . . .
Roger *Everyone* works for this company.
Michael I can't do this to my own father.
Roger Well, look at it this way, Herbert: if this one's your father, the next one won't be!
Michael People aren't raw materials. You can't just bundle them about like this.
Roger It was your idea to reduce the work force.
William And a super idea it was, too.
Michael But look what happens when you put these bright ideas into practice. My dad gets the sack!
William You can't have your bone and eat it!
Roger What about our profits?
Michael Your profits—bollocks!
Roger What did you say?
Michael I said . . . I resign.

William Biting the hand that feeds him.
Roger I think we'd better call a constable.

Roger and William exit with the sack

Fantasy ends

George If I'd had the opportunities in life you've had, Michael, I certainly wouldn't be sitting about six months after leaving University, with no job. It makes nonsense of everything. It's not as though there weren't any jobs to be had either. I don't know why you didn't take that personnel manager's job. I know it wasn't exactly what you had in mind but it was a bloody good opening.
Michael I couldn't have done that.
George Your generation—you've had it all given you on a plate. You think you can pick and choose like the world owes you a living. When I was your age, I was married, there was a war on, you had to look after yourself. You did what you were told.

George exits

Michael turns upstage, opens his briefcase, turns, takes out The Golden Pathway Annual, *throws it away* C *and exits*

The Lights fade to Black-out

CURTAIN

FURNITURE AND PROPERTY LIST

Please read the Production Notes on pages xi-xii NB. Two chairs are on stage throughout

ACT I

Scene 1

Off stage: Suitcase containing a pair of stockings inside an ornamental elephant **(George)**

ACT I

Scene 2

Off stage: Nil

ACT I

Scene 3

Off stage: Nil

ACT I

Scene 4

Off stage: Briefcase, questionnaire clipboard with pen, card and leaflet **(Collins)**
Cup and saucer **(Enid)**

ACT I

Scene 5

Off stage: Saucepan (**Enid**)

ACT I

Scene 6

Off stage: Birthday cake with 5 lighted candles **(Enid)**
Gift-wrapped *Golden Pathway Annual*, newspaper **(George)**
Fire bucket, stirrup pump **(Stage Management)**

ACT I

SCENE 7

Off stage: Cup and saucer **(June)**

ACT I

SCENE 8

Off stage: Box of hats **(Miss Jones, Michael** and **Owen**)
Empty school milk bottle **(Michael)**

ACT I

SCENE 9

Personal: **George:** cigar butt in pocket

ACT I

SCENE 10

Off stage: Two deckchairs **(George)**

ACT I

SCENE 11

Personal: **Enid:** practice papers

ACT I

SCENE 12

Off stage: Picnic basket containing serviettes and three practical torches, dry-cleaning ticket **(William)**

Personal: **Roger:** plaster cast in pocket

ACT II

SCENE 1

Off stage: Rulers and textbooks **(Michael** and **Owen)**

ACT II

SCENE 2

Off stage: Nil

ACT II

SCENE 3

Off stage: Nil.

ACT II

SCENE 4

Off stage: Nil

ACT II

SCENE 5

Off stage: Cane **(The Head)**

Personal: **Michael:** blood sac

ACT II

SCENE 6

Off stage: Nil

ACT II

SCENE 7

Off stage: Nil

ACT II

SCENE 8

Personal: **George:** lighted cigarette

ACT II

SCENE 9

Off stage: Paint brushes and buckets **(Michael** and **Girl Friend)**

ACT II

SCENE 10

Off stage: Two glasses **(George)**

ACT II

Scene 11

Personal: **Michael:** briefcase containing *The Golden Pathway Annual*

ACT II

Scene 12

Personal: **George:** sack

LIGHTING PLOT

Property fittings required: nil

Various simple interior and exterior settings

ACT I

To open: Full general lighting

Cue 1	**Enid:** "Oh George, I do love you." *Black-out*	(Page 4)
Cue 2	**George:** "Hang on." *Snap on full general lighting*	(Page 4)
Cue 3	**Enid:** ". . . by selling brooms." *Lighting change for fantasy sequence*	(Page 9)
Cue 4	To open SCENE 7 *Change to full general lighting*	(Page 11)
Cue 5	To open SCENE 12 *Lighting change for fantasy sequence*	(Page 21)
Cue 6	**William:** ". . . our swimming things with us." *Fade to black-out*	(Page 25)
Cue 7	**George** turns the lights on *Snap on full general lighting*	(Page 25)
Cue 8	**George** and **Michael** exit *Black-out*	(Page 25)

ACT II

To open: Full general lighting

Cue 9	**Mademoiselle:** ". . . la vie française" *Lighting change for fantasy sequence*	(Page 33)
Cue 10	To open SCENE 6 *Change to full general lighting*	(Page 36)
Cue 11	To open SCENE 12 *Lighting change for fantasy sequence*	(Page 46)
Cue 12	**Roger** and **William** exit with the sack *Change to full general lighting*	(Page 48)
Cue 13	**Michael** exits *Fade to black-out*	(Page 48)

EFFECTS PLOT

ACT I

Cue 1 They switch on their torches (Page 25)
Owl hoot

Cue 2 They follow cautiously (Page 25)
Glass crash

ACT II

Cue 3 **Michael** "And still I lived . . ." (Page 29)
Electric school bell

Cue 4 **Lady** (off): "Top flat, come up." (Page 29)
Automatic door buzz

MADE AND PRINTED IN GREAT BRITAIN BY
LATIMER TREND & COMPANY LTD PLYMOUTH

MADE IN ENGLAND